THE PRISONER OF ZENDA

ANTHONY HOPE was the pen name of Anthony Hope Hawkins (1863–1933). He was born in Clapton in London in 1863, where his father, the Reverend Edwards Comerford Hawkins, was headmaster of St John's Foundation School for the Sons of Poor Clergy. His mother, Jane Isabella Hawkins, née Grahame, was the aunt of banker and author Kenneth Grahame. Hope shone as a student at Marlborough College and went on to Balliol College, Oxford, graduating with a first-class honours degree in 'Greats' (Literae Humaniores). President of the Oxford Union, he excelled in debate, and went on to train as a barrister, hoping ultimately to enter politics. In his spare time he wrote fiction, with modest results until *The Prisoner of Zenda* (1894) and its 1898 sequel, *Rupert of Hentzau*, made his reputation. None of his later work achieved the same level of commercial and critical success, but stage and later film adaptations kept his name before the public, and brought in considerable revenue. During the First World War he served at what later became the Ministry of Information at Wellington House, and was knighted for his work in 1918. For health reasons he rented and later bought Heath Farm in Surrey, where he died in 1933.

NICHOLAS DALY is Professor of Modern English and American Literature at University College Dublin, and a member of the Royal Irish Academy. His publications include the monographs *Modernism, Romance, and the Fin de Siècle* (1999), *Literature, Technology and Modernity* (2004), *Sensation and Modernity in the 1860s* (2009), *The Demographic Imagination and the Nineteenth-Century City: Paris, London, New York* (2015), and *Ruritania: A Cultural History* (Oxford University Press, 2020). For Oxford World's Classics he has also edited Baroness Orczy's *The Scarlet Pimpernel*.

T0060988

OXFORD WORLD'S CLASSICS

*For over 100 years Oxford World's Classics have brought
readers closer to the world's great literature. Now with over
700 titles—from the 4,000-year-old myths of Mesopotamia to the
twentieth century's greatest novels—the series makes available
lesser-known as well as celebrated writing.*

*The pocket-sized hardbacks of the early years contained
introductions by Virginia Woolf, T. S. Eliot, Graham Greene,
and other literary figures which enriched the experience of reading.
Today the series is recognized for its fine scholarship and
reliability in texts that span world literature, drama and poetry,
religion, philosophy and politics. Each edition includes perceptive
commentary and essential background information to meet the
changing needs of readers.*

OXFORD WORLD'S CLASSICS

ANTHONY HOPE

The Prisoner of Zenda

Edited with an Introduction and Notes by
NICHOLAS DALY

OXFORD
UNIVERSITY PRESS

OXFORD
UNIVERSITY PRESS

Great Clarendon Street, Oxford, OX2 6DP,
United Kingdom

Oxford University Press is a department of the University of Oxford.
It furthers the University's objective of excellence in research, scholarship,
and education by publishing worldwide. Oxford is a registered trade mark of
Oxford University Press in the UK and in certain other countries

First published as a World's Classics paperback 1994
Reissued as an Oxford World's Classics paperback 2001, 2009
New edition 2020

Impression: 1

Published in the United States of America by Oxford University Press
198 Madison Avenue, New York, NY 10016, United States of America

British Library Cataloguing in Publication Data
Data available

Library of Congress Control Number: 2019948777

ISBN 978-0-19-884109-8

Printed and bound in Great Britain by
Clays Ltd, Elcograf S.p.A.

CONTENTS

INTRODUCTION

*Those who do not wish to know details of the plot may prefer to read
the Introduction as an Afterword.*

FEW novels have had the impact of Anthony Hope's *The Prisoner of
Zenda*, which inspired hit plays, created a whole new subgenre of
popular narrative, and went on to a long afterlife on the screen.
Published in 1894, Hope's bestselling novel tells the story of an
English gentleman, Rudolf Rassendyll, who stumbles into political
intrigue and romance while holidaying in the small German-speaking
state of Ruritania. A lookalike for the Ruritanian king, he is persuaded
to impersonate the incapacitated King Rudolf at his coronation in
order to thwart the political schemes of the king's half-brother.
However, matters become more complex when the real king is kidnapped, and Rassendyll finds himself falling in love with Princess
Flavia. Swashbuckling abounds, and the novel culminates in the daring rescue of the real king from the Castle of Zenda, after which
Rassendyll must reveal the truth to Flavia. The fast-paced novel
quickly inspired lucrative stage versions in the US and Britain and
became something of a sensation: you could play the *Prisoner of Zenda*
board game and dance to the *Zenda* waltzes, and there were even
towns named Zenda. Copycat stories soon appeared, so many that by
the early 1900s critics began to recognize the 'Ruritanian romance' as
a new subgenre of pocket-kingdom adventure. Raymond P. Wallace
describes these as 'Cardboard Kingdom' novels, and writers as diverse
as P. G. Wodehouse, John Buchan, and Frances Hodgson Burnett
tried their hand at the form. Through the cinema these fictional state-
lets also became a significant component of later international popular culture, so that by the end of the twentieth century there was
a long, long list of Ruritanian stories set in such tinsel territories as
Alaine, Alasia, Axphain, Balaria, Barovia, Bomania, Bovinia, Cadonia,
Carpathia, Dawsbergen, Freedonia, Grand Fenwick, Graustark,
Hohenwald, Karaslavia, Livonia, Mervo, Metavania, Novia, Panoplia,
Sylvania, Thermosa, and Wallaria.

Anthony Hope Hawkins

It is unlikely that the young barrister Anthony Hope Hawkins (1863–1933) expected any of this when he came up with his colourful story, and it was a curious twist of fate for a young man who seemed destined for a career at the Bar and in politics. He was born in Clapton in London in 1863 into a family that had produced a long line of doctors, lawyers, and clergymen. His father, the Reverend Edwards Comerford Hawkins, was headmaster of St John's Foundation School for the Sons of Poor Clergy, and later vicar of St Bride's church on Fleet Street; his mother, Jane Isabella Hawkins, née Grahame, was the aunt of banker and author Kenneth Grahame. After Marlborough College, Anthony went on to Balliol College, Oxford, where his contemporaries included Lord Curzon (future viceroy of India), Edward Grey (later a leading Liberal politician), L. T. Hobhouse (who became an academic and major theorist of Liberalism), J. A. Spender (future editor of the *Westminster Gazette*), Cosmo Lang (future Archbishop of York, and of Canterbury), and Charles Mallet, later Sir Charles Mallet (Liberal politician and Hawkins's biographer). Hawkins excelled as a student and shone at debate, president at different times of both the Russell Club and the Oxford Union, so although an academic fellowship eluded him, a bright career seemed assured. Like most young barristers Hawkins had some lean years in the beginning, but he survived, partly through work from his cousin, Sir Henry 'Hanging' Hawkins, a High Court judge; he also tested the waters of politics, running unsuccessfully as the Liberal candidate for Wycombe in Buckinghamshire. In his spare time he wrote fiction under the name Anthony Hope. The young barrister's first novel, *A Man of Mark* (1890), published at his own expense, was a semi-comic tale set in the fictional Aureataland, a deeply corrupt Latin American republic. He wrote three more novels in this period, as well as short stories, and a successful serial about a long-running flirtation, 'The Dolly Dialogues', that appeared in the *Westminster Gazette*. One of the short stories, 'Sport Royal', looks forward to *Zenda*. Its wry narrator, British traveller Julius Jason, is visiting Heidelberg when he is mistaken for a Colonel Despard, and drawn into the affairs of the prince and princess of the fictional Glottenberg. When he crosses the princess, she stabs him in a fit of temper. Not seriously injured, he keeps the dagger as a memento of his adventure. The story lacks the narrative drive and high romance of *Zenda*, but mistaken identity, Germanic royal intrigue, and breezy, first-person narration are all present.

While his early work was by no means ignored by critics, it was *Zenda* that made Anthony Hope's name. Walking back on 28 November 1893 from Westminster County Court to his chambers in Brick Court, Middle Temple, he came up with the idea of a more complex story of lookalikes set in another German principality. Soon he had the name Ruritania, and within a month he had written a draft of the novel. The Bristol publisher J. W. Arrowsmith accepted the manuscript, and in April 1894 it appeared alongside such books as Jerome K. Jerome's *Three Men in a Boat* (1889) in their light fiction series, retailing at three shillings and sixpence. Its success was such that the young barrister gave up the law, and became a full-time writer; Anthony Hawkins was replaced by Anthony Hope. Money from the novel itself and its sequel, *Rupert of Hentzau* (1898), from successful stage adaptations, and from American lecture tours, made him comfortably off, able to afford a substantial house in Bedford Square when he married American Elizabeth Somerville Sheldon in 1903. Even in later years, when his new novels were no longer greeted quite so eagerly, revenue continued to accrue from film versions of *Zenda*. When Hawkins died in 1933 he was remembered in his *Times* obituary as the inventor of 'Ruritania, a country of his imagination in the Balkans . . . and thus the father of the many romantic stories that have since entertained lovers of gaily-coloured fiction'.[1] (By then it had been forgotten that the original Ruritania was a German state rather than the Balkan kingdom it had become in the work of many of his later imitators.)

The Novel

In *The Prisoner of Zenda* we enter the world of daydream right from the start, since our narrator hero, Rudolf Rassendyll, is the 6-foot

---

[1] 'Sir Anthony Hope Hawkins: The Creator of Ruritania', *The Times*, 10 July 1933.

2-inch younger brother of an English earl who is also, he confesses, a good shot and a capable swordsman with a cool head, and he 'can ride anything that ha[s] a back to sit on' (p. 8). Among other languages he speaks fluent German, having attended a German school and university. With an income of £2,000 a year, he is very comfortable indeed (a senior white-collar worker in this period might have earned £500 a year, and a labourer something closer to £50). Through the indiscretions of an eighteenth-century ancestress, our hero also happens to be distantly related to the ruling family of Ruritania, and has inherited the long straight nose and dark red hair of the Elphbergs. At a loose end, Rassendyll privately resolves to visit Ruritania to see the forthcoming coronation of his namesake, King Rudolf, since not only is it a country etched in his own family history, but it is also 'a highly interesting and important kingdom, one which had played no small part in European history, and might do the like again under the sway of a young and vigorous ruler, such as the new king was rumoured to be' (p. 9). It is a description somewhat at odds with the impression of Ruritania that we form later, since the country seems small and inward-looking, its king bibulous and weak. En route he stops off at Paris, where the German statelet is also in the air: he meets an old friend, Bertram Bertrand, who has fallen for an attractive widow, Madame Antoinette de Mauban, though she cares for someone far grander, Michael, Duke of Strelsau, half-brother to the King of Ruritania. Rassendyll travels by train to Ruritania, changing at Dresden, which gives us some idea of the country's location. But to avoid the coronation crowds in the capital he leaves the train just over the frontier in Zenda, some 50 miles from Strelsau. Zenda is where the Duke of Strelsau has his estate, and Rassendyll learns that 'Black Michael', as he is known, is fiercely jealous of his half-brother, not only for his crown, but because he is likely to marry Princess Flavia, their cousin.

It is at this point that Rassendyll's adventures begin in earnest: napping in the forest of Zenda, and dreaming that he is married to Princess Flavia, he wakes to find himself an object of much interest to two men, Colonel Sapt and Fritz von Tarlenheim, who turn out to be in the service of the king. Elements of his dream linger, since when King Rudolf appears he happens to be the mirror image of our hero, though Rassendyll is a shade taller, and has a beard. When the king is drugged that night by a bottle of wine sent by Duke Michael as a coronation gift, Colonel Sapt boldly proposes that Rassendyll should take his Highness's place in the coronation, for if the king is not crowned Michael is poised to seize control of Ruritania. (The veteran Sapt, loyal but eminently pragmatic, is one of Hope's greatest creations, and a prominent character in all adaptations of *Zenda* for the stage and screen.) The king has been abroad too much to be well known to most people, and their resemblance is uncanny. The Englishman is nothing loth, and the novel quickly sets aside any practical barriers to the impersonation: Sapt gives the now clean-shaven Rassendyll some quick lessons in court etiquette and in the Roman Catholic service used for the coronation. Riding through the streets of Strelsau, the ersatz king cuts a dashing figure in the dazzling uniform that becomes a part of most subsequent versions of *Zenda*: 'Perhaps I ought to say that I was all dressed in white, except my boots [and] I wore a silver helmet with gilt ornaments' (p. 33). But it is when they reach the cathedral that he faces the real test in the form of Princess Flavia and Michael:

At last we were at the Cathedral. Its great grey front, embellished with hundreds of statues and boasting a pair of the finest oak doors in Europe, rose for the first time before me, and the sudden sense of my audacity almost overcame me. Everything was in a mist as I dismounted. I saw the Marshal and Sapt dimly, and dimly the throng of gorgeously robed priests who awaited me. And my eyes were still dim as I walked up the great nave, with the pealing of the organ in my ears. I saw nothing of the brilliant throng that filled it, I hardly distinguished the stately figure of the Cardinal as he rose from the archiepiscopal throne to greet me. Two faces only stood out side by side clearly before my eyes—the face of a girl, pale and lovely, surmounted by a crown of the glorious Elphberg hair (for in a woman it is glorious), and the face of a man, whose full-blooded red cheeks, black hair, and dark deep eyes told me that at last I was in presence of my brother, Black Michael. And when he saw me his red cheeks went pale all in a moment, and his helmet fell with a clatter on the floor. Till that moment I believe that he had not realised that the King was in very truth come to Strelsau. (p. 34)

The scheme works—even the Titian-haired Flavia takes him for her intended.

So far, so good. However, Rassendyll's situation becomes more complicated when the real king is kidnapped by Michael and held in the castle of Zenda. If the castle is stormed, Michael's men will kill the king, and throw him down 'Jacob's Ladder', a pipe leading to the moat. Smitten by Flavia, and finding that she is not indifferent, the Englishman is briefly tempted to continue in his regal role indefinitely. But honour trumps desire, and he, Sapt, and Fritz scheme to rescue the king, aided by Madame de Mauban, who has her own reasons for thwarting Michael's designs on the throne. Swashbuckling action is always to the fore, and there are lively clashes with Michael's swordsmen, in one of which Rassendyll is wounded by Rupert of Hentzau, Michael's dashing but amoral young henchman.

Hentzau is an important part of the novel's moral scheme, as like the real king he is a double for Rassendyll. They share a certain reckless courage, a love of action and adventure, and they both see themselves as ladies' men: Rassendyll kisses his landlady's daughter before he ever meets Flavia, and Hentzau is known as a breaker of hearts. But where our hero largely cleaves to a knightly code, Hentzau is completely corrupt. When he encounters Rassendyll riding with Flavia, he offers to betray Michael in exchange for the player-king's reward:

'—Black Michael will fall, like the dog he is; the prisoner, as you call him, will go by Jacob's Ladder—ah, you know that!—to hell! Two men will be left—I, Rupert Hentzau, and you, the King of Ruritania.'

He paused, and then, in a voice that quivered with eagerness, added:

'Isn't that a hand to play?—a throne and your princess! And for me, say a competence and your Majesty's gratitude.'

'Surely,' I exclaimed, 'while you're above ground, hell wants its master!'

'Well, think it over,' he said. 'And, look you, it would take more than a scruple or two to keep me from yonder girl,' and his evil eye flashed again at her I loved.

'Get out of my reach!' said I; and yet in a moment I began to laugh for the very audacity of it. (p. 105)

Hentzau, then, is a charming devil. But the reader can see that he is also something less palatable, particularly in his relations with women. Early on we are told that he is a 'handsome villain, and the gossip ran that many a lady had troubled her heart for him' (p. 83). But later we learn that he 'my Lord Rupert would choose [killing] sooner for a pastime than any other—ay, sooner than he would ruin a woman, though that he loves also' (p. 93). And when we discover that he plans to possess Madame de Mauban with or without her consent, we wonder how much force may have been involved in his previous dealings with women. To Rassendyll Rupert seems a debonair daredevil, the most charismatic of his enemies, but the novel also allows us to see him as a sexual predator. Either way we sense that there will have to be a reckoning between the two, if Rassendyll's better self, and his chivalric values, are to prevail.

The Englishman's daring infiltration of the castle to save the imprisoned king provides the narrative climax, and becomes a set piece in subsequent stage and film adaptations. Modern weaponry is largely set aside, as we see in this passage, in which Rassendyll has just killed one of Michael's guard, Bersonin, and now must fence for his life against Detchard, a hired English blade:

We were sword to sword. By blessed chance, neither he nor Bersonin had been wearing their revolvers. I found them afterwards, ready loaded, on the mantelpiece of the outer room: it was hard by the door, ready to their hands, but my sudden rush in had cut off access to them. Yes, we were man to man: and we began to fight, silently, sternly, and hard. Yet I remember little of it, save that the man was my match with the sword—nay, and more, for he knew more tricks than I; and that he forced me back against the bars that guarded the entrance to 'Jacob's Ladder.' And I saw a smile on his face, and he wounded me in the left arm.

No glory do I take for that contest. I believe that the man would have mastered me and slain me, and then done his butcher's work, for he was the most skilful swordsman I have ever met (p. 124)

Partly through luck, the player king prevails, and the real king is saved, though Rupert of Hentzau manages to escape to fight another day. The duel between Rassendyll and his evil double ends prematurely, the showdown postponed until the novel's sequel, which is named for Hentzau.

Having toyed with some fairy-tale elements, in the end Hope denies us a fairy-tale ending: Rassendyll and Flavia must part, she to marry the real king. Hope makes of their parting a highly emotional set piece:

'Your ring will always be on my finger, your heart in my heart, the touch of your lips on mine. But you must go, and I must stay. Perhaps I must do what it kills me to think of doing.'

. . .

There struck on our ears the sound of singing. The priests in the chapel were singing masses for the souls of those who lay dead. They seemed to chant a requiem over our buried joy, to pray forgiveness for our love that would not die. The soft, sweet, pitiful music rose and fell as we stood opposite one another, her hands in mine.

'My queen and my beauty!' said I.

'My lover and true knight!' she said. 'Perhaps we shall never see one another again. Kiss me, my dear, and go!'

I kissed her as she bade me; but at the last she clung to me, whispering nothing but my name, and that over and over again—and again—and again; and then I left her. (p. 144)

The three-month king returns to live a quiet country life in England, but still feels that some day he may 'mix again in great affairs' (p. 151). Every year he goes to Dresden, where his old comrade-in-arms Fritz brings him a gift from her: a single rose, and the message 'Rudolf—Flavia—always' (p. 152). While giving us a strong sense of an ending, the stage is also set for the sequel, *Rupert of Hentzau*.

The critics enthused over Hope's heady cocktail of the contemporary and the historical, *The Times* comparing him to Alexandre Dumas *père*, and praising the way he planted 'a medieval romance in the civilization of the nineteenth century'; it advised readers that 'no tale of adventure in far-off, mysterious countries surpasses the strange excitements [of] this story of the three months spent by an English gentleman in the petty kingdom of Ruritania, in Germany'.[2] *The Academy* also saw the French connection, and enthusiastically greeted this '*roman de cape et d'épée*' (sword and cape novel).[3] The *Pall Mall Gazette* saw it as an updated Arthurian tale: 'The hero of this brilliant little extravaganza is no medieval knight errant, but a thoroughly modern young man about town . . . yet the adventures which befall him would put those of "Arthur's Knights" into the shade'.[4] American

[2] 'Recent Novels', *The Times*, 21 May 1894.
[3] 'New Novels', *The Academy*, 2 June 1894.
[4] 'Reviews: Two Novels', *Pall Mall Gazette*, 22 May 1894.

reviewers too were reminded of Dumas, with the *New York Times* noting that it 'was a clever man who could take Porthos, Athos, Aramis and D'Artagnan out of their seventeenth century uniforms and clothe them in shooting jackets and knickerbockers'.[5] Nor was the book-buying public any less captivated. *Zenda* sold briskly in its first few months, and by the end of the year it was *the* bestselling book in Britain.[6] A bestseller, when that term was just coming into use, it also continued to sell steadily for decades.[7] By 1933 Arrowsmith's had sold 300,000 copies in Britain, and other British publishers disposed of 200,000 in cheaper editions; considerable numbers were sold across the Empire, and there were school editions in India and Egypt. The book was even more successful in various versions in the US where the rights were bought by the firm of Henry Holt, who later derived additional income from newspaper syndication.[8]

Pocket Kingdoms, Sources, and Contexts

In his essay 'Cardboard Kingdoms' Raymond P. Wallace lists a number of what he sees as the key traits of the genre, including 'The Chase' and 'The Duel'. But he begins with the setting, 'The Fictitious Country', which, he adds, is 'preferably small and preferably a monarchy'.[9] It is this qualification that goes to the heart of *The Prisoner of Zenda*'s appeal. At the core of Hope's 'Ruritanian romance' is the Ruritanian territory itself, the chocolate-box kingdom in which Rassendyll's adventures unfold. The use of imaginary countries was nothing new, of course: Thomas More's Utopia, Jonathan Swift's Lilliput and Brobdingnag, and the Brontës' Angria are just some of

---

[5] 'New Publications: A Bright and Stirring Romance', *New York Times*, 27 May 1894; and see also 'Recent Publications', *New Haven Morning Herald*, 11 Oct. 1894.

[6] Based on the 'Monthly Report of the Wholesale Book Trade' (England). See Troy J. Bassett and Christina M. Walter, 'Booksellers and Bestsellers: British Book Sales as Documented by *The Bookman*, 1891–1906', app. 2, *Book History*, 4 (2001), 205–36.

[7] On bestsellers and steady sellers, see Clive Bloom, *Bestsellers: Popular Fiction Since 1900* (2nd edn, Houndmills: Palgrave Macmillan, 2008), 1–5.

[8] In 1905, for instance, the novel was serialized in the *National Tribune* (DC) and other papers.

[9] Raymond P. Wallace, 'Cardboard Kingdoms', *San José Studies*, 13/2 (Spring 1987), 23–34 at 23.

the more famous earlier instances. But Hope's ersatz German kingdom is neither a space for political thought experiments, nor a space of pure fantasy. A short train journey from Dresden, Ruritania is a realistic fictional territory, only mildly exotic to his British readers, who might not have been very surprised if it turned out to exist somewhere among Germany's twenty-six states. Yet the novel also renders the Elphbergs' kingdom a place apart, an adventure-space very different to Dresden, let alone the 305 Park Lane in which the story opens. To use Mikhail Bakhtin's term, the pocket monarchy represents a 'chronotope', a particular narrative arrangement of time and space.[10] Ruritania's very name suggests that we will be stepping out of the modern world into a more rural or pastoral territory, though of course it turns out to provide a very lively form of pastoral escape. The country's small size is by no means incidental to the appeal of the adventure, and not only because it serves to make our hero's actions loom all the larger. Its sequestered and contained nature also imparts to the story a particular intimacy, a cosiness even, and we know that these adventures will have no consequences outside Ruritania's borders, except in Rudolf's broken heart; what happens in Ruritania really does stay there. In his 1973 history of science fiction, *Billion Year Spree*, Brian Aldiss describes some strains of the post-apocalyptic novel as offering 'cosy catastrophes'; Anthony Hope, it might be argued, launches a tradition of cosy adventure. Of course this should also remind us of the nature of fiction itself: part of the power of the novelist is that he or she provides contained worlds for our enjoyment, page-bound territories securely contained within their covers.

As original as it is, Hope's Ruritanian lively adventure is not without precedent. Hope's stirring tale owes something to his earlier 'Sport Royal' and the court of Glottenberg. But he was also drawing upon other writers, and perhaps more surprisingly, upon the musical stage. The composers of operetta early on realized the narrative usefulness of bijou fictional Germanic states. Jacques Offenbach's 1867 *La Grande-Duchesse de Gérolstein*, for instance, centres on the wilful Grand Duchess of a petty German state who wreaks havoc when she

---

[10] See M. M. Bakhtin, *The Dialogic Imagination: Four Essays*, trans. Caryl Emerson and Michael Holquist (Austin: University of Texas Press, 1981).

falls madly in love with one of her soldiers; its comic complications and bright melodies delighted the crowds who had flocked to Paris for that year's Exposition Universelle. In fleshing out his fictional world Hope's debts are to the other novelists of the period who had popularized the tale of swashbuckling adventure. The writer who had done most in this line in this was Robert Louis Stevenson, whose *Treasure Island* (1883) and *Kidnapped* (1886) had driven the late Victorian 'revival of romance', a turn away from the everyday world of the domestic novel towards colourful novels of swordplay and derring-do, stirring tales that recalled the children's literature of earlier decades, as well as the work of the elder Alexandre Dumas. This switch from stories of family and courtship to those of manly action also characterizes the work of H. Rider Haggard, whose novels of African adventure included *King Solomon's Mines* (1885) and *She* (1887). The now less familiar Stanley J. Weyman covered similar ground in such historical swashbucklers as *A Gentleman of France* (1893) and *Under the Red Robe* (1894). *The Prisoner of Zenda* borrows ingredients from all of these. From Stevenson and Weyman he takes the resourceful hero who is good with a sword in his hand, and behind Rudolf Rassendyll we can catch glimpses of Stevenson's Alan Breck and Weyman's Gaston de Bonne. From Weyman too, perhaps, comes the chivalric love interest, though in this respect Hope is drawing also upon a much older tradition: contemporary reviewers recognized echoes of Arthurian tales of the Round Table. Haggard for his part had shown him that novels of action and adventure do not need to be set in the past, as long as you can devise a setting in which heroic action is plausible. *She* and *King Solomon's Mines* took English readers all the way to the plains of Africa, but Hope realized that an out-of-the-way pocket European kingdom might do just as well. These are not Hope's only sources, of course. As he himself pointed out, confused identity is a common theme in the very earliest stories, and a staple of English comedy from Shakespeare on.[11] Closer to his own time there was something of a flurry of tales of doubles and of changing places, Mark Twain's *The Prince and the Pauper* (1881) being a well-known example. Among less familiar instances are F. Anstey's comic novel of 1882,

---

[11] Hope, *Memories and Notes* (New York: Doubleday, Doran, 1928), 112.

Vice Versa, in which a son and his father switch bodies; a great success in its day, it was also the source of a hit play. We might even note the parallel between Hope's use of doubles and the work of one of his most famous contemporaries, Oscar Wilde, a leading figure in the late Victorian aesthetic movement. In Wilde's *The Picture of Dorian Gray* the central character effectively changes places with his own portrait, and Wilde would return to the idea of the exchangeability of identity in *The Importance of Being Earnest* (1895).

However, the comparison also indicates how removed Hope's tale is from aestheticism and similar intellectual fare. *Dorian Gray* is really an exercise in style rather than plot, and represents a fictional recasting of the aesthetic ideas expounded by Walter Pater in his *Studies in the History of the Renaissance* (1873). Hope, who like Wilde had a first-class honours degree from Oxford, was scarcely unaware of issues of style, and indeed *Zenda*'s success can in part be attributed to the novel's economic and yet vivid use of language. But the world view that unfolds from *Zenda* is a very different one to that which we associate with Wilde, and with the 1890s more generally. Where Wilde delights in contradictions and in the questioning of received ideas, including ideas of human nature, Hope celebrates a more traditional fictional order: heroes are heroic and villains are villainous; women are beautiful, noble creatures who must be protected; and monarchies are a good thing, and are to be preserved. To this extent *Zenda* represents a conservative pull, a counter-force to Wilde's playful aestheticism. We might also note in passing how different Hope's tale is to the work of contemporary proto-modernists like Henry James and Joseph Conrad, who saw the novel as an artistic mode for the analysis of character and motive rather than a form of light entertainment.

Of course the realm of fiction does not exist in a vacuum, and Hope's bestseller was also shaped by its more general historical context. On closer inspection we see that it is not really a novel about Germany, but about Britain itself. Britain in 1894 was a major imperial power undergoing a second industrial revolution, involving, for instance, developments in the use of electricity, the internal combustion engine, and new recording and communications technologies. Other forms of revolution were in the air as well. In terms of social history this was the era of the 'New Woman', and women were campaigning for the vote, as well as for more access to education and jobs outside the domestic sphere. Industrial workers and other manual labourers were increasingly discontented, and there were a number of major strikes in the 1880s and 1890s. The condition of the urban poor was a topic of the day, and there was widespread interest in the slums of 'Darkest England', as Salvation Army founder William Booth put it in his influential 1890 account, *In Darkest England and the Way Out*. All of these historical factors register in the novel, though not always directly. Thus *Zenda* is not an 'empire novel' in the usual sense in that we never leave Europe. But written at a time when Britain controlled great swathes of the world, with settler colonies in Australia and North America, and colonial possessions in Africa and Asia, the story is informed by imperial consciousness. The insouciant confidence of Rassendyll, the ex-soldier, can be read in these terms, for example. Perhaps we might even consider whether the novel's chivalric ethos is compensatory: fighting here is a game to be played by the rules and not the rapacious struggle for land, markets, and mineral resources that characterized the 'Age of Empire'. Jeffrey Richards observes of the later swashbuckling heroes of the screen that their 'values are the values of the knightly class', and this accurately describes Hope's hero.[12] One of Rudolf's greatest regrets is that he has broken the rules of fair fighting by stabbing one of Michael's minions in his sleep, and he has to reassure himself that 'It is war—and the king's life is the stake' (p. 98). Thus while it is not an empire novel of the kind that Rider Haggard and Kipling were producing in the same period, it does lend itself to analysis in similar terms, as a source of the enabling myths of imperial heroism that have been analysed by such critics as Martin Green, Graham Dawson, and Wendy R. Katz.[13]

In the same way that it skirts any discussion of empire, the novel seems to be determined to turn its back on the technological trappings

[12] Jeffrey Richards, *Swordsmen of the Screen: From Douglas Fairbanks to Michael York* (London: Routledge and Kegan Paul, 1977), 4.

[13] Martin Green, *Dreams of Adventure: Deeds of Empire* (London: Routledge & Kegan Paul, 1980); Graham Dawson, *Soldier Heroes: British Adventure, Empire and the Imagining of Masculinities* (London: Routledge, 1994); Wendy R. Katz, *Rider Haggard and the Fiction of Empire: A Critical Study of British Imperial Fiction* (Cambridge: Cambridge University Press, 2010).

of the modern world, at a time when Britain was a thoroughly industrial society. *Zenda* is not a historical novel, but we find ourselves in a feudal—and seemingly lawless—land in which combat is often along pre-industrial lines, with swords rather than guns to the fore. As reviewers noted, the occasional appearance of the railway seems almost out of place in the novel. Ruritania is a land of the past, unlike Britain, and also unlike the real Germany, which was beginning to outstrip Britain, the workshop of the world, in its use of new industrial technologies.

As to the feminist 'New Women' of the 1890s, they are nowhere to be found in the novel, which instead celebrates the beauty and nobility of the self-sacrificing Princess Flavia, and even Madame de Mauban's loyalty to Michael is portrayed as admirable in its way. At a time, then, when conceptions of masculinity and femininity were becoming more fluid, Hope seems to reassert an older vision of gendered spheres, of heroic manhood and true womanhood. Flavia is far from powerless, but her principal contribution to the action is through renunciation: not only does she give up Rassendyll, but she is also to marry a man she does not love, to close her eyes and think of Ruritania.

Industrial unrest and the controversies over slums are harder to track in the novel, though perhaps we catch a glimpse of them in the description of the class landscape of Strelsau, which with its echoes of Friedrich Engels's account of industrial Manchester in *The Condition of the Working Class in England* (1845) rather undermines the image of Ruritania as a rural idyll:

The city of Strelsau is partly old and partly new. Spacious modern boulevards and residential quarters surround and embrace the narrow, tortuous and picturesque streets of the original town. In the outer circles the upper classes live; in the inner the shops are situated; and, behind their prosperous fronts, lie hidden populous but wretched lanes and alleys, filled with a poverty-stricken, turbulent, and (in large measure) criminal class. (p. 32)

Needless to say, this turbulent urban population are supporters of Michael rather than the king.

One contemporary topic that finds more direct treatment in the novel is the post-Darwinian interest in heredity. After all, Rassendyll is able to pass for the king only because he bears a striking physical resemblance to him, and that is because they are distant cousins. The trademark Elphberg red hair appears in the Rassendyll line every once in a while as a result of Countess Amelia's 1733 affair with a visiting Elphberg prince, and our hero is thus something of a throwback to earlier generations. Contemporary interest in heredity was coloured by the pseudoscientific ideas of such figures as Cesare Lombroso, who saw criminals as survivals of earlier human types, and Max Nordau, whose *Degeneration* argued that modern life itself is damaging to the nerves, this damage being passed onto the next generation as 'hereditary hysteria'.[14] But as the *Saturday Review* observed of *Zenda*: 'That blessed word "Heredity" is likely to occur to the reader of the first few pages; but the thing itself, the pseudoscientific thing, lifts not its horrid head and multiple issues for a single page to chill the romantic spirit.'[15] The novel references 'this heredity we hear so much about' (p. 7), and retains the idea that traits may be inherited, that the past returns in bodily form, but uses it to reassure us that what comes down through the ages is the innate capacity for heroism and not criminality or intellectual feebleness. This theme is accentuated in the stage version of the novel, in which the following exchange takes place between our hero and Bertram Bertrand, who is now the artist friend who accompanies him to Ruritania:

RUDOLF: My dear boy, you are mistaken. Believe me, even in these prosaic days, you may find your heroes and heroines every morning in the newspaper. Heroism, my dear Bertrand, is innate in every bosom, and awaits but the occasion to call it forth.

BERTRAND: Nonsense. Man is a degenerate animal and you are the horrible example.[16]

Of course it is the idle Rudolf who is proved right when he goes on to fight to save the throne of Ruritania, the tiny German kingdom allowing the modern British gentleman to be his true and more valiant self.

Ruritania, then, can be seen to be a looking-glass version of Britain itself, though a more colourful version of the country in which chivalric

---

[14] Max Nordau, *Degeneration* (1892; London: William Heinemann, 1895).
[15] 'Novels and Stories', *Saturday Review*, 26 May 1894.
[16] Harvard typescript of Edward Rose's *The Prisoner of Zenda*, Act 1, p. 25.

masculinity prevails, and in which womanhood is beautiful, true, and noble. If the town harbours pockets of disaffection, most of the populace are loyal subjects of the king, and devoted to their future queen. What comes out of the genetic past is not degeneracy, but old-school daring and resourcefulness. The concerns and anxieties of the 1890s are evoked and aired, all the better to sweep them away.

Sequels, Adaptations

Hope seems to have written his sequel, *Rupert of Hentzau: From the Memoirs of Fritz von Tarlenheim*, not long after the first novel, though it did not appear in print until the end of 1897, when it began as a serial in the *Pall Mall Magazine*, before appearing from Arrowsmith the following July, with illustrations by the American artist Charles Dana Gibson. The action takes place a few years later, and our narrator this time is Fritz rather than Rassendyll. Some readers may guess that this is because the Englishman is not in a position to write his own account, and so it turns out. The action this time is even more in the mould of medieval romance, with Rassendyll, Sapt, and Fritz striving to protect the honour of the queen. When she rashly sends an actual love letter in lieu of her usual terse note, it is stolen by Rupert of Hentzau. Once again our hero must play the king, in an effort to intercept the letter. But when Rupert kills the real king, Rudolf is trapped in his role. Flavia, Sapt, and Fritz all urge him to stay on as ruler, but while he is pondering the right thing to do he is assassinated. While the body of King Rudolf is buried quietly in the graveyard at Zenda, Rudolf Rassendyll, the player king, is interred in the royal vault in the Cathedral of Strelsau, and the queen orders a Latin inscription to be placed over his resting place, which translates as: 'To Rudolf, who reigned lately in this city, and reigns for ever in her heart—QUEEN FLAVIA'.[17] While it did not enjoy the extraordinary success of its original, Rupert of Hentzau was well received, with *The Times* even ranking it above *Zenda*.[18]

---

[17] *Rupert of Hentzau* (Bristol: Arrowsmith, 1898), 384.
[18] 'Rupert of Hentzau', *The Times*, 25 July 1898.

Stage and Film Adaptations

Like many successful novels of the day, *Zenda* was soon adapted for the stage. For this Hope trusted Edward Rose, an experienced theatre hand, who stuck relatively closely to the novel, though he added a prologue in which we see the eighteenth-century duel between the visiting Prince Rudolf and the husband of Countess Amelia, Rassendyll's ancestor. Rose compressed the action to just four settings: the forest of Zenda in Act 1; the Winter Palace at Strelsau in Act 2; the Castle of Tarlenheim in Act 3; and the dungeon of the Castle of Zenda in the final act. Stage Ruritania first appeared not in London but at the Lyceum Theatre in New York, under the auspices of impresario Daniel Frohman.[19] With E. H. Sothern in the triple lead role (as the eighteenth-century Rudolf and the two modern ones) *Zenda* was a great success, though it was Sothern's successor, James K. Hackett, who made it something of a national institution. The athletic Hackett swashbuckled his way through the play thousands of times, and played no small part in the rise of the swordsman as hero on stage and screen: sword in hand 'he first showed that the up-to-date hero must needs be able to exterminate a dozen enemies alone and single-handed'.[20] So successful was Hackett in the part that in 1896 Parker Brothers manufactured a board game based on *Zenda*, the cover illustration featuring a vignette of Hackett as Rassendyll.[21]

On the other side of the Atlantic it was actor-manager George Alexander of the St James's Theatre in London who took up Rose's adaptation; in his hands it became less a swashbuckler than an opulent romantic melodrama, with spectacular costumes and scenery. Evelyn Millard was cast as Princess Flavia, Alexander himself playing the challenging triple role. For the St James's, *Zenda* was something of a departure, since it was a theatre best known for contemporary British comedy and more serious 'problem plays': Oscar Wilde's *Lady*

---

[19] The Frohman brothers, Daniel, Gustave, and Charles, were a major force in American theatre production in these years, and Charles was a member of the Theatrical Syndicate that controlled much of the nation's theatre booking.

[20] 'Extravagant Heroics of New Stage Duels', *San Francisco Call*, 2 Feb. 1902.

[21] This game was re-released with a different cover to exploit the publicity around the 1937 film version of the novel. Parker Brothers' greatest success was *Monopoly* (1935).

Windermere's Fan had debuted there (20 February 1892), as had Arthur
Wing Pinero's society take on the 'fallen woman' play, *The Second Mrs
Tanqueray* (27 May 1893). But the fashionable theatre was in need of
a change of direction and box office success. It had had a disastrous
year in 1895, beginning with Henry James's deeply unpopular *Guy
Domville*. Oscar Wilde's sparkling comedy of mistaken identity, *The
Importance of Being Earnest*, followed, and promised to be a hit, before
its run was cut short when Wilde became enmeshed in the public scandal and the series of trials that would end with his conviction for acts
of gross indecency under the Criminal Law Amendment Act, and
a sentence of two years of hard labour. *Zenda* offered the prospect of
a fresh start, and popular success: Alexander, the self-indulgent Jack
Worthing/Ernest of Wilde's play, would become the heroic and manly
Rudolf Rassendyll/King Rudolf. Where Jack invents another identity
to escape from his duties in the country, Rudolf plays a part to save
a kingdom. Evelyn Millard, who had played the precocious Cecily
Cardew in *Earnest*, underwent a similar sea-change to become the
beautiful and dutiful Princess Flavia. The stage *Zenda* made a matinee
idol of the actor-manager, pictured in his silver helmet and ice-cream
coronation uniform in many a photographer's window, while Millard's
extravagant costumes became an inspiration for that season's debu-
tantes. Such an embrace of 'traditional' roles in the West End seems to
have been what a large part of the public wanted, if the play's success
is any indication. Clement Scott in the *Daily Telegraph*, who was one
of the few critics who disliked the play and its 'cardboard and tinsel'
characters, admitted that there had been 'three or four calls after every
act, cheers for author, double cheers for actors', and that the 'triumph
of America ha[s] been repeated in critical London'.[22] Equally rapturous audiences greeted subsequent performances. All told, the play ran
for 303 performances at the St James's, and a separate touring production brought in the crowds in the provinces. (We might note that in
August a tall and striking young actor, one C. Aubrey Smith, joined
the touring cast in the part of Duke Michael.) The often acerbic
George Bernard Shaw felt that *Zenda* had by the autumn become

---

[22] Clement Scott, '*The Prisoner of Zenda* at the St James's', *Daily Telegraph*, 8 Jan.
1896, p. 5.

'a permanent institution, like Madame Tussaud's'.[23] After the *annus horribilis* of 1895, Alexander found that his turn to the romantic melodrama of *Zenda* had made him both popular and prosperous; when he refurbished the theatre in 1900 he made 'Ruritania' its new telegraphic address.

Zenda played in revivals for many more years before taking a significant role in the rise of the motion picture industry, one of a handful of properties that harnessed the prestige of literature and the theatre for the new medium. The first screen Rudolf Rassendyll was none other than James K. Hackett. By 1913 he was more than weary of the role that had made him famous, but having been declared bankrupt in 1909 he was recruited by film impresario Adolph Zukor who offered him $5,000 to play the part for the camera.[24] The English-born Beatrice Beckley, the second Mrs Hackett, was to be Flavia. Zukor had teamed up with Daniel Frohman to form the Famous Players Film Company (Famous Players would later become Famous Players-Lasky which in turn became Paramount), their plan being to secure a more middle-class audience for the fledgling medium by capturing the best-known stage performers of the day in their signature plays; these would be expensive four-reel features rather than short films. In 1912 Zukor had presented Sarah Bernhardt in the French-made *Queen Elizabeth*; American productions would include James O'Neill in *The Count of Monte Cristo*; Minnie Maddern Fiske in *Tess of the d'Urbervilles*; and Hackett in *The Prisoner of Zenda*. If Zukor's original declared aim was simply to 'embalm' theatrical performances, the end result for *Zenda* was something far more cinematic.[25] Although they followed the play, directors Edwin S. Porter and Hugh Ford also open up the action by including footage of Hackett on horseback, a moat sequence, and a spectacular coronation ball. A sumptuous production by the standards of the day, *The Prisoner of Zenda* premiered on 24 March 1913 at Loew's Theatres in New York, after a private exhibition on 18 February at the Lyceum Theatre,

[23] *Dramatic Opinions and Essays*, ii (New York: Brentano's, 1922), 66.
[24] Zukor, *The Public is Never Wrong* (New York: G. P. Putnam's, 1954), 75–89.
[25] Charles Musser, *Before the Nickelodeon: Edwin S. Porter and the Edison Manufacturing Company* (Berkeley and Los Angeles: University of California Press, 1991), 466.

where Frohman's *Zenda* had debuted in 1895.[26] With ads touting it as 'the greatest artistic achievement ever attained in motion pictures', and 'the greatest love story since Romeo and Juliet', it captured the public's imagination, and became the first successful four-reel American film.[27]

A British-made film, starring the Shakespearean actor Henry Ainley, followed two years later from London Film Productions. It attracted favourable reviews, *The Times*, for instance, suggesting that this screen *Zenda* made for 'a much more dramatic production than the stage could manage, because trick photography introduced the possibility of having the King and Rassendyll before us simultaneously', and the film's success encouraged London Film Productions to produce *Rupert of Hentzau* later that year, again starring Ainley.[28] It was not until 1922 that the classic silent version of the novel appeared, directed by Rex Ingram, born Reginald Hitchcock, a clergyman's son from Ireland who had a major hit the previous year with *The Four Horsemen of the Apocalypse*. Lewis Stone stars as Rudolf and Alice Terry (Mrs Ingram) as Flavia, with Ramon Novarro turning in a charismatic performance as a leering Rupert of Hentzau. By this time Ruritania had moved east in the popular imagination, the Cyrillic signs at Strelsau railway station indicating that we are a long way from the novel's Dresden—presumably after the First World War Germany was no longer in favour as a land of adventure. It is a stylish film, featuring Ingram's trademark lighting effects, fluid action sequences, and some deft comic touches that serve to undercut the chivalric pageantry; in light of the horrors of the war some of the knightly ethos of the original was, perhaps, beginning to wear thin. Nonetheless, Hope (now a knight himself) politely hailed the film at its London premiere as a 'veritable triumph of cinematography'.[29]

If Ingram's fine film is no longer so well known, it is in part because the sound era brought another classic version of *Zenda* (1937),

[26] A print of the film survives in the collection of the George Eastman Museum in Rochester, New York.

[27] Full-page ad, *Moving Picture World*, Jan.–Mar. 1913, p. 431.

[28] 'The Prisoner of Zenda on the Film', *Times*, 10 Mar. 1915.

[29] W.H., 'Notable Film: Success of the "Prisoner of Zenda"', *Pall Mall Gazette*, 30 Jan. 1923, p. 4. Hope had been knighted for his propaganda work during the war.

produced by David O. Selznick. Selznick is most famous for his evocation of the American South in *Gone with the Wind* (1939), but he was also a great Anglophile who had two years earlier produced critically acclaimed versions of Dickens's *David Copperfield* and *A Tale of Two Cities*. For *Zenda* he assembled a starry cast in which British actors predominate: Ronald Colman and Madeleine Carroll play the leads; David Niven appears as Fritz; and Colonel Zapt (*sic*) is none other than the 73-year-old C. Aubrey Smith, whom we last met as Black Michael in the St James's touring production of 1894. Raymond Massey is Black Michael, Myrna Loy is Madame de Mauban, and Douglas Fairbanks Jr plays Rupert with considerable panache. (Fairbanks claimed many years later that his father had insisted he accept the part: 'Take it. That role is actor proof. Lassie could play the part.'[30]) John Cromwell directs, and James Wong Howe produced the meticulous photography, but in his usual way Selznick also asserted his control by drafting in additional expertise: George Cukor for the romantic scenes; W. S. Van Dyke to reshoot the storming of the castle and some of the swordplay. The latter is indeed spectacular; former US Olympic fencer Ralph Faulkner (who plays Bersonin) coached the actors, and doubled for Colman in the more elaborate set-pieces.[31]

The film's appearance in 1937 was far from random, since the Anglophile Selznick seems to have been deeply moved by the coronation crisis of the previous year; perhaps he saw the film as rewriting the story of Edward and Mrs Simpson, with the roles of king and commoner reversed, and duty trumping love. More practically, royalty was in the news, and the 1937 coronation of George VI created splendid opportunities for publicity: Selznick organized an 'international radio hookup . . . saluting Britain's new monarch' on the eve of the 12 May coronation. Fairbanks was MC, accompanied by Carroll, Colman, Massey, Niven, and Aubrey Smith. The programme was broadcast from Los Angeles by NBC, and then 'short-waved to British Broadcasting in London . . . Selznick greet[ing] London on behalf of

[30] Sarah Booth Conroy, 'Star Memories', *Washington Post*, 12 May 1983. *Lassie Come Home* was not released until 1943, so Fairbanks may have been thinking of Rin Tin Tin, an earlier canine star.
[31] See Nick Evangelista, *The Encyclopedia of the Sword* (Westport, CT: Greenwood, 1985), 117–19.

Hollywood and the industry'.[32] Further ballyhoo was to follow: for the New York premiere at Radio City Music Hall in September legendary publicist Russell Birdwell flew in the entire population of Zenda, Ontario; this was, in fact, a surprisingly affordable gesture, as the town had only twelve inhabitants.[33] The public, and the reviewers, were enthusiastic. The *New York Times* was particularly smitten: 'Here', it proclaimed, 'is proper, swashbuckling adventure, set in that vast mythical land (of which Zenda is a province) where honor is brighter, villainy unregenerate and beauty incomparable . . . here is the most pleasing film that has come along in ages'.[34]

The 1937 film was to be the zenith of *Zenda*'s film career. The 1952 Technicolor remake is pleasing to the eye, but it is more style than substance, effectively a shot-by-shot remake of Selznick's film. As *Time* noted, 'Ruritania in this edition is as magnificent a mythical kingdom as MGM money can buy—outsize castles, royal hunting lodges and gargantuan coronation balls'.[35] Again, British actors dominate the cast: Stewart Granger is our hero, Deborah Kerr is Princess Flavia, and James Mason is Rupert; Louis Calhern (Zapt) and Jane Greer (de Mauban) are the principal Americans, though Lewis Stone, the star of the 1922 film, appears in a cameo role. Perhaps the best thing in the film is the gripping sword fight between Rudolf and Rupert, choreographed by the Belgian fencing master Jean Heremans, which is even more spectacular than its predecessors. When the film was playing around the US in early 1953, there was again plenty of free publicity due to the imminent coronation of Elizabeth II: coronation memorabilia filled the shops, and department stores were planning sales of British goods to coincide with the June ceremony.[36]

After the 1950s *Zenda* attracted parody rather than respectful homage, though there were a few exceptions. In the 1961 Bengali film *Jhinder Bandi* (dir. Tapan Sinha), one Gauri Shankar Roy (Uttam

[32] 'NBC, Selznick Plan Coronation Air Show', *Motion Picture Daily*, 24 Apr. 1937, 4.
[33] 'The New Pictures', *Time* 30/11 (13 Sept. 1937), 36.
[34] 'The Screen: The Prisoner of Zenda Opens at the Music Hall', *New York Times*, 3 Sept. 1937.
[35] 'The New Pictures', *Time* 60/18 (3 Nov. 1952), 102.
[36] Frank Prochaska, *The Eagle and the Crown: Americans and the British Monarchy* (New Haven: Yale UP, 2008), 165.

Kumar) becomes involved in adventure and romance in the fictional kingdom of Jhind because of his striking resemblance to the king, but in the end sacrifices his love for Rani Kasturi Bai (Arundhati Devi), and rides off to let the true king reign.[37] *Dr Who*, the long-running BBC science fiction series, produced a homage in the form of the 1978 (Season 16) episode, *The Androids of Tara*, which sets the struggle for the crown on a feudal planet on which androids do the hard work (its working title was *The Androids of Zenda*).[38] But the more general tendency was to mine Ruritania for laughs. The 1965 comedy *The Great Race*, for instance, features a *Zenda* sequence set in Carpania that culminates not in a thrilling duel, but in a cream-pie fight. The second of George MacDonald Fraser's comic historical novels, *Royal Flash* (1970), features a plot that turns on the resemblance of the rackety Harry Flashman to a Danish prince engaged to a German princess; Richard Lester's film adaptation followed in 1975, with Malcolm McDowell in the lead, and Oliver Reed as the scheming Otto von Bismarck. Also in 1975 the *Carry On* comedy team made *The Prisoner of Spenda*, an episode of their *Carry on Laughing* Thames Television series, in which Count Yerkackers and Count Yackoff enlist the help of one Arnold Basket (Sid James) to save the throne of Pluritania. But the major cannibalization of Hope's story for laughs was the 1979 Peter Sellers *Prisoner of Zenda*, in which Sellers plays three parts: the aged Rudolf IV; his son, the fast-living Rudolf V; and the latter's lookalike, stoic London cabman Syd Frewin; Lynne Frederick (Mrs Sellers) is Princess Flavia. It is a slapstick version of earlier films in which there are comic moments, but not enough of them: that Rudolph of Ruritania cannot pronounce the letter 'r' is a fair specimen of the kind of entertainment it offers. Sellers himself was deeply dissatisfied with the final cut, and in a morning talk show interview actually warned people to avoid the film.[39] Although it did not lose money, it was scarcely a success, and reviewers suggested that *Zenda* had at last had its day. As

---

[37] Its direct source was a novel of the same name by Bengali writer Sharadindu Bandyopadhyay.

[38] See the online BBC guide to classic episodes of the series: http://www.bbc.co.uk/doctorwho/classic/episodeguide/androidsoftara/detail.shtml.

[39] Walter Mirisch, *I Thought We Were Making Movies, Not History* (Madison: University of Wisconsin Press, 2008), 353–5.

Judith Martin put it in the *Washington Post*: 'It's time to let *The Prisoner of Zenda* go. It's wrong to make one novel go through the trial of becoming a movie five times, and the new attempt only creates useless suffering.'[40] Producers may have taken this to heart: with the exception of a low-budget television version in 1984, little attempt has been made to return to Ruritania.

Generic Influence

If one of *The Prisoner of Zenda*'s legacies has been a long series of adaptations, the other has been the emergence of a whole new subgenre of Ruritanian adventure stories. Other writers were soon drawn to Hope's Ruritanian formula, and by 1901 there were already accounts of 'Ruritanian romance' as a recognizable form.[41] Early British examples include Sydney C. Grier's *An Uncrowned King* (1896), Samuel Gordon's *The Queen's Quandary* (1903), and Percy Brebner's *Princess Maritza* (1906); while American instances include Richard Harding Davis's *The Princess Aline* (1895), Harold McGrath's *Arms and the Woman* (1899), and George Barr McCutcheon's *Graustark: The Love Behind a Throne* (1901).[42] Devil-may-care protagonists found adventure in such territories as Gerisau, Ehrenfelberstein, Hohenphalia, Montara, Grimland, Montalba, and Scarvania. Comic variants included P. G. Wodehouse's *The Prince and Betty* (1912), set on the small island of Mervo. The trend lingered in the interwar years, perhaps in part because real pocket kingdoms and real royals were in much shorter supply, since the Romanovs, Hohenzollerns, Habsburgs, and smaller royal fry had been ushered off the stage of history. Interwar Ruritanias reborn include Dornford Yates's Riechtenburg in *Blood Royal* and *Fire Below* (1929 and 1930), and John Buchan's Evallonia in *The House of the Four Winds* (1935).[43]

---

[40] ' "Zenda" Out In the Fifth', *Washington Post*, 25 May 1979.

[41] The term 'Ruritanian romance' appears early on in, for instance, 'Amusements', *The Sphere*, Saturday, 4 May 1901, p. 28; and 'Literature and Art', *Sheffield Daily Telegraph*, Wednesday, 8 Apr. 1903, p. 3.

[42] Grier was the pseudonym of Hilda Caroline Gregg.

[43] Clive Bloom suggests that Hope's novels 'create the style for the escapist adventure set within an international political crisis' (*Bestsellers*, 170).

Of all of these, it is McCutcheon's *Graustark* and its sequels that enjoyed the greatest popularity right across the first quarter of the century, outselling *Zenda* itself in this period. In these variants of the formula, plucky young American men and women find adventure and eligible royals in the mountainous kingdom of Graustark and its neighbouring territories. For instance, in the second in the series, *Beverly of Graustark* (1904), a resourceful young American woman travels to Graustark and falls for a handsome but penniless man of the mountains, only to find that he is really Prince Dantan of Dawsbergen. At a time when real American 'dollar princesses' were marrying into aristocratic European families, these light-hearted fantasies enjoyed enormous success; stage and film versions followed, though after the Second World War the world of Graustark failed to attract new readers, and the series is now largely forgotten.[44]

When the pure strain of 'Ruritanian romance' went out of fashion, elements of it continued to pop up in fiction. We find more than a hint of it in, for instance, Leslie Charteris's *The Last Hero* and *Knight Templar* (both 1930); Ford Madox Ford's *Vive Le Roy* (1937); and Vladimir Nabokov's *Pale Fire* (1962). Ruritanias began to appear in other fictional forms too, including children's fiction, science fiction, and classic interwar detective fiction; for example, Frances Hodgson Burnett's Samavia, in *The Lost Prince* (1915); Hergé's Syldavia, in *King Ottokar's Sceptre*, one of Tintin's adventures (1938); Robert Heinlein's Mars in *Double Star* (1956); and Margery Allingham's Averna in *Sweet Danger* (1933). Elsewhere we see Hope's influence on the spectacular West End musical theatre of Ivor Novello (e.g. Krasnia, in *Glamorous Night*, 1935). After the Second World War, just when we might expect the old recipe to have lost its residual potency, it was reinvented to deal with the new geopolitical order, and we see a clutch of Cold War narratives set in such pocket territories as Barovia, Lichtenburg, Concordia, and Gaillardia. Perhaps the best-known of these is Grand Fenwick, the comic duchy of Leonard Wibberley's *The Mouse That Roared* (1955, filmed 1959), which faces down the atomic superpowers.

[44] Films included *Beverly of Graustark* (1914 and 1926), *Graustark* (1915 and 1925), and *The Prince of Graustark* (1916).

With the fall of the Iron Curtain these latter-day Ruritanias lost their role. However, there is life in the old formula still. In 2000 the American writer Meg Cabot published *The Princess Diaries*, the first in a bestselling series of comic novels for the Young Adult market. Cabot's heroine, Mia Thermopolis, is a 14-year-old high school student who lives with her mother and their cat, Fat Louie, in a loft apartment in Greenwich Village; her father lives overseas, in a small francophone country called Genovia, somewhere on the Riviera, 'between France and Italy'.[45] Mia thinks he is a politician, but visiting New York he reveals to Mia that he is actually Prince Phillipe (*sic*) of Genovia, and she herself is Amelia Mignonette Grimaldi Thermopolis Renaldi, Crown Princess of Genovia, while her formidable *grand-mère* is the Princess Dowager. The novel's vogue was further boosted by the Disney film adaptations that followed in 2001 and 2004, featuring Anne Hathaway as Mia and Julie Andrews as her Genovian grandmother. The *Diaries*' extraordinary success on page and screen is complexly related to the rise of contemporary 'princess culture', the fascination with princesses among young girls, adeptly exploited by the manufacturers of clothes, accessories, and indeed films. How does *The Princess Diaries* relate to the Ruritanian strain that descends from *The Prisoner of Zenda*? Genovia is clearly a pocket kingdom in the Ruritanian line, with more than an added dash of Monaco, Prince Phillipe clearly being modelled on Prince Albert.[46] Mia is not an impersonator like Rudolf Rassendyll, though; more closely resembling Beverly in *Beverly of Graustark*, Mia is transformed from being a fairly ordinary young American into a real American princess. However, the core fantasy has changed in the intervening years, since Mia's royal status does not depend on her marrying a European prince—she simply is a princess.

In turn, the success of the Disneyfied *Diaries* spawned a new subgenre of films that once again trades in the fascination with picturesque pocket kingdoms, and in which American heroines find love and tiaras in increasingly unlikely chocolate-box European principalities. Hallmark has produced *A Royal Christmas* (2014, Cordinia), *A Crown*

---

[45] Meg Cabot, *The Princess Diaries* (New York: HarperTeen, 2000), 26.
[46] As the press revealed in 1992, Albert does, in fact, have an American daughter, Jazmin.

for Christmas (2015, Winshire), *Christmas at the Palace* (2018, San Senova), and *Royal Matchmaker* (2018, Voldavia), while streaming media content-provider Netflix has entered the war for Christmas viewers with *A Christmas Prince* (2017, Aldovia), *A Christmas Prince: The Royal Wedding* (2018, also Aldovia), and *The Princess Switch* (2018, Belgravia). Ruritanian motifs survive in these films—mistaken identities, royal romance, court pageantry in the form of a coronation, or at least a court ball—but there is usually scope too for Christmas sleigh rides and open fires, and romantic interest almost wholly displaces adventure.

As for the country that gave birth to Ruritania, at the time of writing no such revival is under way, and the term Ruritanian has largely come to possess a pejorative sense, less evocative of picturesque adventure than of petty states, hidebound by tradition and protocols, and excessively fond of spectacle and braid. For instance, the prospect of Britain's exit from the European Union led some commentators to point out that aspects of the country were distinctly Ruritanian, or to argue that the country as a whole was sleepwalking into a Ruritanian future. According to the *Financial Times* people were wondering in 2017 'how Britain had so quickly descended from a self-confident, economically successful world power into a country more closely resembling Ruritania'.[47] It is always unwise to speculate about where popular culture is going next, but in light of such commentary, it seems unlikely that we are on the cusp of a British revival of *Zenda*-style romantic adventure.

In the meantime, of course, we have Anthony Hope's classic novel to enjoy. If its references to red hair and heredity are now a little opaque, the story itself retains all its fast-paced appeal. And Ruritania itself, perhaps the greatest of fictional pocket kingdoms, seems just as fresh as when the young barrister Anthony Hawkins dreamed it up in 1893.

[47] George Parker and Alex Barker, 'Intrigue and Betrayal Stalk UK's Corridors of Power', *Financial Times*, 1 July 2016.

NOTE ON THE TEXT

THIS edition follows Tony Watkins's 1994 Oxford World's Classics edition, which was reset from the first edition published by J. W. Arrowsmith in 1894.

SELECT BIBLIOGRAPHY

Biographical Sources

Hope, Anthony, *Memories and Notes* (London: Hutchinson, 1927).
Mallet, Sir Charles, *Anthony Hope and His Books, Being the Authorized Life of Sir Anthony Hope Hawkins* (London: Hutchinson, 1935).

Critical Sources

Barton, Ruth, *Rex Ingram: Visionary Director of the Silent Screen* (Lexington: University Press of Kentucky, 2014).
Bloom, Clive, *Bestsellers: Popular Fiction Since 1900* (2nd edn, Houndmills: Palgrave Macmillan, 2008).
Goldsworthy, Vesna, *Inventing Ruritania: The Imperialism of the Imagination* (1998; London: C. Hurst and Co., 2013).
Green, Martin, *Dreams of Adventure: Deeds of Empire* (London: Routledge & Kegan Paul, 1980).
Harding, James, *Ivor Novello: A Biography* (1987; Cardiff: Welsh Academic Press, 1997).
Kaplan, Amy, 'Romancing the Empire: The Embodiment of American Masculinity in the Popular Historical Novel of the 1890s', *American Literary History*, 2/4 (Winter, 1990), 659–90.
Kestner, Joseph A., *Masculinities in British Adventure Fiction, 1880–1915* (London: Routledge, 2016).
Lazarus, A. L., and Jones, Victor H., *Beyond Graustark: George Barr McCutcheon, Playwright Discovered* (Port Washington, NY: Kennicat Press, 1981).
Macqueen-Pope, W., *St. James's, Theatre of Distinction* (London: W. H. Allen, 1958).
Mason, A. E. W., *Sir George Alexander and the St. James's Theatre* (London: Macmillan, 1935).
Morrow, Charles, 'It's Good to be the King: Hollywood's Mythical Monarchies, Troubled Republics, and Crazy Kingdoms', in Andrew Horton and Joanne E. Rapf (eds), *A Companion to Film Comedy* (Chichester: Wiley Blackwell, 2012), 251–72.
Niemeyer, Paul J., 'The Royal Red-Headed Variant: *The Prisoner of Zenda* and the 1893 Heredity Debates', *College Literature*, 42/1 (Winter 2015), 112–38.
Richards, Jeffrey, *Swordsmen of the Screen: From Douglas Fairbanks to Michael York* (London: Routledge and Kegan Paul, 1977).

Shuler, 'Raising (Razing?) Princess: Autoethnographic Reflections on Motherhood and The Princess Culture', *Popular Culture Studies Journal*, 3/1–2 (2015), 458–86.

Thomson, David, *Showman: The Life of David O. Selznick* (London: André Deutsch, 1993).

Wallace, Raymond P., 'Cardboard Kingdoms', *San José Studies*, 13/2 (Spring 1987), 23–34.

Watkins, Tony, 'Introduction', *The Prisoner of Zenda* (Oxford: Oxford World's Classics, 1994).

A CHRONOLOGY OF ANTHONY HOPE

	Life	Literary and Cultural Background	Historical Background
1863	(9 Feb.) Born at Clapton House, Hackney, London, to Jane Isabella Hawkins (née Grahame) and the Reverend Edwards Comerford Hawkins, headmaster of St John's Foundation School for the Sons of Poor Clergy.	Death of William Makepeace Thackeray.	First London underground railway line opens.
1872	The Foundation School and the Hawkins family move to Leatherhead, Surrey.	Joseph Sheridan Le Fanu, *In a Glass Darkly*	Britain introduces the secret ballot for parliamentary and local government elections.
1876	Enters Marlborough College, the public school that his father had attended. He excels academically and in debating and sports, and edits the school magazine.	George Eliot, *Daniel Deronda*	Alexander Graham Bell patents a form of telephone.
1881	Enters Balliol College, Oxford, on an exhibition (later increased to a scholarship). Becomes active in college debating, and contributes to the new *Oxford Magazine*.	Henry James, *Portrait of a Lady*; Mark Twain, *The Prince and the Pauper*	President Garfield assassinated in the US.
1885	Graduates with First Class Honours in 'Greats' (Literae Humaniores).	H. Rider Haggard, *King Solomon's Mines*	The Berlin Conference concludes.
1886	President of the Oxford Union. Moves to London, where he lives with his father, now vicar of St Bride's in Fleet Street.	R. L. Stevenson, *The Strange Case of Dr Jekyll and Mr Hyde*; *Kidnapped*	The Benz Motorwagen is patented.

	Life	Literary and Cultural Background	Historical Background
1887	Called to the Bar. Acquires chambers at 1 Brick Court, in Middle Temple. Writes short pieces for newspapers and magazines.	Arthur Conan Doyle's first Sherlock Holmes story, *A Study in Scarlet*, appears in *Beeton's Christmas Annual*. H. Rider Haggard, *She*	Fire at the Theatre Royal in Exeter, the worst theatre fire in British history.
1890	As 'Anthony Hope', publishes at his own expense his first novel, *A Man of Mark*.	Oscar Wilde's *The Picture of Dorian Gray* appears in *Lippicott's Magazine*.	The Wounded Knee massacre in South Dakota.
1891	(Oct.) *Father Stafford* published. By the end of the year it had sold 199 copies.	Thomas Hardy, *Tess of the d'Urbervilles*	Death of Charles Stewart Parnell, influential Irish politician.
1892	(Mar.) *Mr Witt's Widow*. (July) Runs unsuccessfully as Liberal candidate for South Buckinghamshire.	*Lady Windermere's Fan* premieres at the St James's Theatre in London.	Ellis Island opens as an immigration station in New York.
1893	*A Change of Air*; *Sport Royal and Other Stories*; 'The Dolly Dialogues' serialized in the *Westminster Gazette*.	Arthur Wing Pinero's *The Second Mrs Tanqueray* produced by George Alexander at the St James's Theatre.	Coup against Queen Lili'uokalani in Hawaii.
1894	(Apr.) *The Prisoner of Zenda* becomes a critical and commercial success. Hope becomes a full-time writer, with A. P. Watt as his agent. *The God in the Car*	Stanley Weyman, *Under the Red Robe*	Death of Tsar Alexander III.
1895	(Sept.) Edward Rose's adaptation of *Zenda* first produced at the Lyceum in New York. *The Chronicles of Count Antonio*	H. G. Wells, *The Time Machine*; Oscar Wilde, *The Importance of Being Earnest*	Lumière brothers exhibit cinematograph in Paris.

	Life	Literary and Cultural Background	Historical Background
1896	(Jan.) George Alexander's production of *Zenda* at the St James's in London. Parker Brothers produce a board game version of *Zenda*. *The Heart of Princess Osra and Other Stories*	First production of Anton Chekhov's *The Seagull*.	The Jameson Raid in the South African Republic ends in victory for the Boers.
1897	*Phroso*; reading tour of the US. (Dec.) *The Adventure of Lady Ursula* staged in Philadelphia; *Rupert of Hentzau* begins serialization in the *Pall Mall Magazine*	Bram Stoker, *Dracula*	J. J. Thomson's experiments with electrons.
1898	*Rupert of Hentzau*. (Oct.) *The Adventure of Lady Ursula* staged at Duke of York's Theatre in London. (Nov.) *Rupert of Hentzau* premieres in Philadelphia.	Oscar Wilde, *The Ballad of Reading Gaol*	Spanish–American war.
1899	(Oct.) George Alexander's production of *Hentzau* opens in Glasgow. *The King's Mirror*	Joseph Conrad's *Heart of Darkness* serialized.	Philippine–American war begins.
1900	*Quisanté*. Alexander's *Hentzau* fails to please in London. Elected Chairman of the Committee of the Society of Authors. Production of *English Nell*, adapted from *Simon Dale*.	L. Frank Baum, *The Wonderful Wizard of Oz*	Boxer Uprising in China.
1901	*Tristram of Blent*	*The Hound of the Baskervilles* begins serialization in the *Strand*. Kipling, *Kim*	Death of Queen Victoria.
1902	*Pilkerton's Peerage* (Garrick Theatre). *The Intrusions of Peggy*	A. E. W. Mason, *The Four Feathers*	End of the second Anglo-Boer War.

	Life	*Literary and Cultural Background*	*Historical Background*
1903	Second reading tour of the US. Marries Elizabeth (Betty) Somerville Sheldon, a young American, and takes a house on London's Bedford Square. New York production of *Captain Dieppe*.	G. B. Shaw, *Man and Superman*	Wright brothers' first flight at Kitty Hawk; Emmeline Pankhurst founds WSPU (Women's Social and Political Union).
1905	*A Servant of the Public*	Edgar Wallace, *Four Just Men*; Edith Wharton, *The House of Mirth*	Aliens Act restricts immigration into Britain.
1906	*Sophy of Kravonia*	John Galsworthy, *The Man of Property*	Alfred Dreyfus cleared of treason in France.
1907	*Tales of Two People*; *The Great Miss Driver*	Joseph Conrad, *The Secret Agent*	Romanian peasants' uprising.
1910	*Helena's Path* produced. *Second String*	Post-Impressionist exhibition at the Grafton Galleries in London.	Edward VII dies, and George V becomes king.
1913	Adolph Zukor produces the first film version of *The Prisoner of Zenda*, starring James K. Hackett, and directed by Edwin S. Porter.	Armory Show of modern art in New York.	Victoriano Huerta becomes president of Mexico after a military coup.
1914	At Wellington House Hope works on propaganda pamphlets for what later becomes the Ministry of Information.	Joyce, *Dubliners*	First World War begins.
1915	British films of *Zenda* and *Hentzau*, featuring Henry Ainley. Hope finds the *Hentzau* 'very good indeed'. For health reasons he rents and later buys Heath Farm in Surrey.	D. H. Lawrence, *The Rainbow*; D. W. Griffith, *The Birth of a Nation*	First Zeppelin raids on Britain.

	Life	Literary and Cultural Background	Historical Background
1916	*Sofia di Kravonia*, Italian film of Hope's novel.	Ronald Firbank, *Inclinations*	(Apr.) The Easter Rising in Ireland.
1917	Moves from Bedford Square to smaller house in Gower Street.	Norman Douglas, *South Wind*	(Feb. and Oct.) Revolutions in Russia.
1918	Knighted for his war work.	Gustav Holst, *The Planets*	End of First World War.
1919	*An Adventure in Hearts*, film based on *Captain Dieppe*.	E. M. Hull, *The Sheik*	Paris Peace Conference begins.
1920	Film version of *Sophy of Kravonia*. *Lucinda*	F. Scott Fitzgerald, *This Side of Paradise*	(1919–20) First 'Red Scare' in US.
1922	Rex Ingram's version of *Zenda*; *Possession*, a film based on *Phroso*.	T. S. Eliot, *The Waste Land*; Joyce, *Ulysses*; Virginia Woolf, *To the Lighthouse*	Mussolini's march on Rome.
1923	Victor Heerman's film of *Hentzau*.	Sigmund Freud, *The Ego and the Id*	Calvin Coolidge becomes president of the United States.
1925	*Little Tiger*, his last novel. *Princess Flavia*, Sigmund Romberg's operetta version of *Zenda*.	Woolf, *Mrs Dalloway*	Mussolini tightens his grip on power in Italy.
1927	*Memories and Notes*	Fritz Lang, *Metropolis*	Charles Lindbergh flies from New York to Paris.
1928		John Logie Baird demonstrates colour television pictures.	Voting age for women lowered from 30 to 21 in Britain.
1933	(8 July) Dies at Heath Farm.	George Orwell, *Down and Out in Paris and London*	Hitler becomes chancellor in Germany.
1937	David O. Selznick's film of *Zenda*, with Robert Donat, Madeleine Carroll and Douglas Fairbanks Jnr.	John Steinbeck, *Of Mice and Men*	Bombing of Guernica during Spanish Civil War.

	Life	Literary and Cultural Background	Historical Background
1949	Lux Radio Theatre version of *Zenda*, with the voice of Ronald Colman.	Carol Reed, *The Third Man*	USSR successfully explodes atomic bomb.
1952	Technicolor remake of *Zenda*, with Stewart Granger and Deborah Kerr.	*The Diary of Anne Frank* published in English translation.	Mau Mau campaign in Kenya. Elizabeth II succeeds her father, George VI.
1961	*Jhinder Bandi*, Bengali film loosely based on *Zenda*.	Joseph Heller, *Catch-22*	Yuri Gagarin is first person in space.
1964	BBC TV series of *Hentzau*.	Ian Fleming, *Chitty-Chitty-Bang-Bang: The Magical Car*	Malawi gains independence.
1975	*The Prisoner of Spenda*, Carry On team parody of *Zenda* for Thames Television.	E. L. Doctorow, *Ragtime*	Vietnam War ends.
1979	Peter Sellers appears in comic version of *Zenda*, dir. Richard Quine.	Caryl Churchill, *Cloud 9*	Iran becomes an Islamic Republic when the Shah is deposed.
1984	BBC television series of *Zenda*.	William Gibson, *Neuromancer*	First Apple Macintosh personal computer on sale.
1988	Animated television film based on *Zenda* made by Burbank Films Australia.	David Henry Hwang, *M. Butterfly*	Iran–Iraq War ends.
2000	Meg Cabot, *The Princess Diaries*	Zadie Smith, *White Teeth*	Vladimir Putin becomes president of Russia.

THE PRISONER OF ZENDA

CONTENTS

CHAPTER I

THE RASSENDYLLS—WITH A WORD ON THE ELPHBERGS

'I WONDER when in the world you're going to do anything, Rudolf?' said my brother's wife.

'My dear Rose,' I answered, laying down my egg-spoon, 'why in the world should I do anything? My position is a comfortable one. I have an income nearly sufficient for my wants (no one's income is ever quite sufficient, you know): I enjoy an enviable social position: I am brother to Lord Burlesdon, and brother-in-law to that most charming lady, his countess. Behold, it is enough!'

'You are nine-and-twenty,' she observed, 'and you've done nothing but——'

'Knock about? It is true. Our family doesn't need to do things.'

This remark of mine rather annoyed Rose, for everybody knows (and therefore there can be no harm in referring to the fact) that, pretty and accomplished as she herself is, her family is hardly of the same standing as the Rassendylls. Besides her attractions, she possessed a large fortune, and my brother Robert was wise enough not to mind about her ancestry. Ancestry is, in fact, a matter concerning which the next observation of Rose's has some truth.

'Good families are generally worse than any others,' she said.

Upon this I stroked my hair: I knew quite well what she meant.

'I'm so glad Robert's is black!' she cried.

At this moment Robert (who rises at seven and works before breakfast) came in. He glanced at his wife: her cheek was slightly flushed; he patted it caressingly.

'What's the matter, my dear?' he asked.

'She objects to my doing nothing and having red hair,' said I, in an injured tone.

'Oh! of course he can't help his hair,' admitted Rose.

'It generally crops out once in a generation,' said my brother. 'So does the nose. Rudolf has got them both.'

'I wish they didn't crop out,' said Rose, still flushed.

'I rather like them myself,' said I, and, rising, I bowed to the portrait of Countess Amelia.

My brother's wife uttered an exclamation of impatience.

'I wish you'd take that picture away, Robert,' said she.

'My dear!' he cried.

'Good heavens!' I added.

'Then it might be forgotten,' she continued.

'Hardly—with Rudolf about,' said Robert, shaking his head.

'Why should it be forgotten?' I asked.

'Rudolf!' exclaimed my brother's wife, blushing very prettily.

I laughed, and went on with my egg. At least I had shelved the question of what (if anything) I ought to do. And, by way of closing the discussion—and also, I must admit, of exasperating my strict little sister-in-law a trifle more—I observed:

'I rather like being an Elphberg myself.'

When I read a story, I skip the explanations; yet the moment I begin to write one, I find that I must have an explanation. For it is manifest that I must explain why my sister-in-law was vexed with my nose and hair, and why I ventured to call myself an Elphberg. For eminent as, I must protest, the Rassendylls have been for many generations, yet participation in their blood of course does not, at first sight, justify the boast of a connection with the grander stock of the Elphbergs or a claim to be one of that Royal House. For what relationship is there between Ruritania and Burlesdon, between the Palace at Strelsau or the Castle of Zenda and Number 305 Park Lane, W.?*

Well then—and I must premise that I am going, perforce, to rake up the very scandal which my dear Lady Burlesdon wishes forgotten—in the year 1733, George II sitting then on the throne, peace reigning for the moment, and the king and the Prince of Wales being not yet at loggerheads, there came on a visit to the English Court a certain prince, who was afterwards known to history as Rudolf the Third of Ruritania. The prince was a tall, handsome young fellow, marked (may be marred, it is not for me to say) by a somewhat unusually long, sharp and straight nose, and a mass of dark-red hair—in fact, the nose and the hair which have stamped the Elphbergs time out of mind. He stayed some months in England, where he was most courteously received; yet, in the end, he left rather under a cloud. For he fought a duel (it was considered highly well-bred of him to waive all question of his rank) with a nobleman, well known in the society of the day, not only for his own merits, but as the husband of a very beautiful wife. In that duel Prince Rudolf received a severe wound, and, recovering therefrom, was adroitly smuggled off by the Ruritanian ambassador, who had found him a pretty handful. The nobleman was not wounded in the duel; but the morning being raw and damp on the occasion of the meeting, he contracted a severe chill, and, failing to throw it off, he died some six months after the departure of Prince Rudolf, without having found leisure to adjust his relations with his wife—who, after another two months, bore an heir to the title and estates of the family of Burlesdon. This lady was the Countess Amelia, whose picture my sister-in-law wished to remove from the drawing-room in Park Lane; and her husband was James, fifth Earl of Burlesdon and twenty-second Baron Rassendyll, both in the peerage of England, and a Knight of the Garter. As for Rudolf, he went back to Ruritania, married a wife, and ascended the throne, whereon his progeny in the direct line have sat from then till this very hour—with one short interval. And, finally, if you walk through the picture-galleries at Burlesdon, among the fifty portraits or so of the last century-and-a-half, you will find five or six, including that of the sixth earl, distinguished by long, sharp, straight noses and a quantity of dark-red hair; these five or six have also blue eyes, whereas among the Rassendylls dark eyes are the commoner.

That is the explanation, and I am glad to have finished it: the blemishes on honourable lineage are a delicate subject, and certainly this heredity we hear so much about* is the finest scandal-monger in the world; it laughs at discretion, and writes strange entries between the lines of the 'Peerages'.

It will be observed that my sister-in-law, with a want of logic that must have been peculiar to herself (since we are no longer allowed to lay it to the charge of her sex), treated my complexion almost as an offence for which I was responsible, hastening to assume from that external sign inward qualities of which I protest my entire innocence; and this unjust inference she sought to buttress by pointing to the uselessness of the life I had led. Well, be that as it may, I had picked up a good deal of pleasure and a good deal of knowledge. I had been to a German school and a German University,* and spoke German as readily and perfectly as English; I was thoroughly at home in French; I had a smattering of Italian and enough Spanish to swear by. I was, I believe, a strong, though hardly a fine, swordsman and a good shot. I could ride anything that had a back to sit on; and my head was as cool a one as you could find, for all its flaming cover. If you say that I ought to have spent my time in useful labour, I am out of Court and have nothing to say, save that my parents had no business to leave me two thousand pounds a year* and a roving disposition.

'The difference between you and Robert,' said my sister-in-law, who often (bless her!) speaks on a platform, and oftener still as if she were on one, 'is that he recognises the duties of his position, and you only see the opportunities of yours.'

'To a man of spirit, my dear Rose,' I answered, 'opportunities are duties.'

'Nonsense!' said she, tossing her head; and after a moment she went on: 'Now, here's Sir Jacob Borrodaile offering you exactly what you might be equal to.'

'A thousand thanks!' I murmured.

'He's to have an Embassy in six months, and Robert says he is sure that he'll take you as an *attaché*. Do take it, Rudolf—to please me.'

Now, when my sister-in-law puts the matter in that way, wrinkling her pretty brows, twisting her little hands, and growing wistful in the eyes, all on account of an idle scamp like myself, for whom she has no natural responsibility, I am visited with compunction. Moreover, I thought it possible that I could pass the time in the position suggested with some tolerable amusement. Therefore I said:

'My dear sister, if in six months' time no unforeseen obstacle has arisen, and Sir Jacob invites me, hang me if I don't go with Sir Jacob!'

'Oh, Rudolf, how good of you! I am glad!'

'Where's he going to?'

'He doesn't know yet; but it's sure to be a good Embassy.'

'Madame,' said I, 'for your sake I'll go, if it's no more than a beggarly Legation. When I do a thing, I don't do it by halves.'

My promise, then, was given; but six months are six months, and seem an eternity, and, inasmuch as they stretched between me and my prospective industry (I suppose *attachés* are industrious; but I know not, for I never became *attaché* to Sir Jacob or to anybody else), I cast about for some desirable mode of spending them. And it occurred to me suddenly that I would visit Ruritania. It may seem strange that I had never visited that country yet; but my father (in spite of a sneaking fondness for the Elphbergs, which led him to give me, his second son, the famous Elphberg name of Rudolf) had always been averse from my going, and, since his death, my brother, prompted by Rose, had accepted the family tradition which taught that a wide berth was to be given to that country. But the moment Ruritania had come into my head I was eaten up with curiosity to see it. After all, red hair and long noses are not confined to the House of Elphberg, and the old story seemed a preposterously insufficient reason for debarring myself from acquaintance with a highly interesting and important kingdom, one which had played no small part in European history, and might do the like again under the sway of a young and vigorous ruler, such as the new king was rumoured to be. My determination was clinched by reading in *The Times* that Rudolf the Fifth was to be crowned at Strelsau in the course of the next three weeks, and that great magnificence was to mark the occasion. At once I made up my mind to be present, and began my preparations. But, inasmuch as it has never been my practice to furnish my relatives with an itinerary of my journeys and in this case I anticipated opposition to my wishes, I gave out that I was going for a ramble in the Tyrol*—an old haunt of mine—and propitiated Rose's wrath by declaring that I intended to study the political and social problems of the interesting community which dwells in that neighbourhood.

'Perhaps,' I hinted darkly, 'there may be an outcome of the expedition.'

'What do you mean?' she asked.

'Well,' said I, carelessly, 'there seems a gap that might be filled by an exhaustive work on——'

'Oh! will you write a book?' she cried, clapping her hands. 'That would be splendid, wouldn't it, Robert?'

'It's the best of introductions to political life nowadays,' observed my brother, who has, by the way, introduced himself in this manner several times over. *Burlesdon on Ancient Theories and Modern Facts* and *The Ultimate Outcome, by a Political Student*, are both works of recognised eminence.

'I believe you are right, Bob, my boy,' said I.

'Now promise you'll do it,' said Rose earnestly.

'No, I won't promise; but if I find enough material, I will.'

'That's fair enough,' said Robert.

'Oh! material doesn't matter,' she said, pouting.

But this time she could get no more than a qualified promise out of me. To tell the truth, I would have wagered a handsome sum that the story of my expedition that summer would stain no paper and spoil not a single pen. And that shows how little we know what the future holds; for here I am, fulfilling my qualified promise, and writing, as I never thought to write, a book—though it will hardly serve as an introduction to political life, and has not a jot to do with the Tyrol.

Neither would it, I fear, please Lady Burlesdon, if I were to submit it to her critical eye—a step which I have no intention of taking.

CHAPTER II

CONCERNING THE COLOUR OF MEN'S HAIR

IT was a maxim of my Uncle William's that no man should pass through Paris without spending four-and-twenty hours there. My uncle spoke out of a ripe experience of the world, and I honoured his advice by putting up for a day and a night at 'The Continental'* on my way to—the Tyrol. I called on George Featherly at the Embassy, and we had a bit of dinner together at Durand's,* and afterwards dropped in to the Opera; and after that we had a little supper, and after that we called on Bertram Bertrand, a versifier of some repute and Paris correspondent to *The Critic*.* He had a very comfortable little suite of rooms, and we found some pleasant fellows smoking and talking. It struck me, however, that Bertram himself was absent and in low spirits, and when everybody except ourselves had gone, I rallied him on his moping preoccupation. He fenced with me for a while, but at last, flinging himself on a sofa, he exclaimed:

'Very well; have it your own way. I am in love—infernally in love!'

'Oh, you'll write the better poetry,' said I, by way of consolation.

He ruffled his hair with his hand and smoked furiously. George Featherly, standing with his back to the mantel-piece, smiled unkindly.

'If it's the old affair,' said he, 'you may as well throw it up, Bert. She's leaving Paris to-morrow.'

'I know that,' snapped Bertram.

'Not that it would make any difference if she stayed,' pursued the relentless George. 'She flies higher than the paper-trade, my boy!'

'Hang her!' said Bertram.

'It would make it more interesting for me,' I ventured to observe, 'if I knew who you were talking about.'

'Antoinette Mauban,' said George.

'De Mauban,' growled Bertram.

'Oho!' said I, passing by the question of the *de*, 'You don't mean to say, Bert——?'

'Can't you let me alone?'

'Where's she going to?' I asked, for the lady was something of a celebrity.

George jingled his money, smiled cruelly at poor Bertram, and answered pleasantly:

'Nobody knows. By the way, Bert, I met a great man at her house the other night—at least, about a month ago. Did you ever meet him—the Duke of Strelsau?'

'Yes, I did,' growled Bertram.

'An extremely accomplished man, I thought him.'

It was not hard to see that George's references to the duke were intended to aggravate poor Bertram's sufferings, so that I drew the inference that the duke had distinguished Madame de Mauban by his attentions. She was a widow, rich, handsome, and, according to repute, ambitious. It was quite possible that she, as George put it, was flying as high as a personage who was everything he could be, short of enjoying strictly royal rank: for the duke was the son of the late King of Ruritania by a second and morganatic marriage,* and half-brother to the new king. He had been his father's favourite, and it had occasioned some unfavourable comment when he had been created a duke, with a title derived from no less a city than the capital itself. His mother had been of good, but not exalted, birth.

'He is not in Paris now, is he?' I asked.

'Oh no! He's gone back to be present at the king's coronation; a ceremony which, I should say, he'll not enjoy much. But, Bert, old man, don't despair! He won't marry the fair Antoinette—at least, not unless another plan comes to nothing. Still, perhaps, she——' He paused and added, with a laugh: 'Royal attentions are hard to resist—you know that, don't you, Rudolf?'

'Confound you!' said I; and rising, I left the hapless Bertram in George's hands and went home to bed.

The next day George Featherly went with me to the station, where I took a ticket for Dresden.*

'Going to see the pictures?' asked George, with a grin.

George is an inveterate gossip, and had I told him that I was off to Ruritania, the news would have been in London in three days and in Park Lane in a week. I was, therefore, about to return an evasive answer, when he saved my conscience by leaving me suddenly and darting across the platform. Following him with my eyes, I saw him lift his hat and accost a graceful, fashionably dressed woman who had just appeared from the booking-office. She was, perhaps, a year or two over thirty, tall, dark, and of rather full figure. As George talked, I saw her glance at me, and my vanity was hurt by the thought that, muffled in a fur-coat and a neck-wrapper (for it was a chilly April day) and wearing a soft travelling-hat pulled down to my ears, I must be looking very far from my best. A moment later, George rejoined me.

'You've got a charming travelling companion,' he said. 'That's poor Bert Bertrand's goddess, Antoinette de Mauban, and, like you, she's going to Dresden—also, no doubt, to see the pictures. It's very queer, though, that she doesn't at present desire the honour of your acquaintance.'

'I didn't ask to be introduced,' I observed, a little annoyed.

'Well, I offered to bring you to her; but she said, "Another time." Never mind, old fellow, perhaps there'll be a smash, and you'll have a chance of rescuing her and cutting out the Duke of Strelsau!'

No smash, however, happened, either to me or to Madame de Mauban. I can speak for her as confidently as for myself; for when, after a night's rest in Dresden, I continued my journey, she got into the same train. Understanding that she wished to be let alone, I avoided her carefully, but I saw that she went the same way as I did to the very end of my journey, and I took opportunities of having a good look at her, when I could do so unobserved.

As soon as we reached the Ruritanian frontier (where the old officer who presided over the Custom House favoured me with such a stare that I felt surer than before of my Elphberg physiognomy), I bought the papers, and found in them news which affected my movements. For some reason, which was not clearly explained and seemed to be something of a mystery, the date of the coronation had been suddenly advanced, and the ceremony was to take place on the next day but one. The whole country seemed in a stir about it, and it was evident that Strelsau was thronged. Rooms were all let and hotels overflowing; there would be very little chance of my obtaining a lodging, and I should certainly have to pay an exorbitant charge for it. I made up my mind to stop at Zenda, a small town fifty miles short of the capital, and about ten from the frontier. My train reached there in the evening;

I would spend the next day, Tuesday, in a wander over the hills, which were said to be very fine, and in taking a glance at the famous Castle, and go over by train to Strelsau on the Wednesday morning, returning at night to sleep at Zenda.

Accordingly at Zenda I got out, and as the train passed where I stood on the platform, I saw my friend Madame de Mauban in her place; clearly she was going through to Strelsau, having, with more providence than I could boast, secured apartments there. I smiled to think how surprised George Featherly would have been to know that she and I had been fellow-travellers for so long.

I was very kindly received at the hotel—it was really no more than an inn—kept by a fat old lady and her two daughters. They were good, quiet people, and seemed very little interested in the great doings at Strelsau. The old lady's hero was the duke, for he was now, under the late king's will, master of the Zenda estates and of the Castle, which rose grandly on its steep hill at the end of the valley, a mile or so from the inn. The old lady, indeed, did not hesitate to express regret that the duke was not on the throne, instead of his brother.

'We know Duke Michael,' said she. 'He has always lived among us; every Ruritanian knows Duke Michael. But the king is almost a stranger; he has been so much abroad, not one in ten knows him even by sight.'

'And now,' chimed in one of the young women, 'they say he has shaved off his beard, so that no one at all knows him.'

'Shaved his beard!' exclaimed her mother. 'Who says so?'

'Johann, the duke's keeper. He has seen the king.'

'Ah, yes. The king, sir, is now at the duke's shooting-lodge in the forest here; from here he goes to Strelsau to be crowned on Wednesday morning.'

I was interested to hear this, and made up my mind to walk next day in the direction of the lodge, on the chance of coming across the king. The old lady ran on garrulously:

'Ah! and I wish he would stay at his shooting—that and wine (and one thing more) are all he loves, they say,—and suffer our duke to be crowned on Wednesday. That I wish, and I don't care who knows it.'

'Hush, mother!' urged the daughters.

'Oh, there's many to think as I do!' cried the old woman stubbornly. I threw myself back in my deep arm-chair, and laughed at her zeal.

'For my part,' said the younger and prettier of the two daughters, a fair, buxom, smiling wench, 'I hate Black Michael! A red Elphberg for me, mother! The king, they say, is as red as a fox or as——'

And she laughed mischievously as she cast a glance at me, and tossed her head at her sister's reproving face.

'Many a man has cursed their red hair before now,' muttered the old lady—and I remembered James, fifth Earl of Burlesdon.

'But never a woman!' cried the girl.

'Ay, and women, when it was too late,' was the stern answer, reducing the girl to silence and blushes.

'How comes the king here?' I asked, to break an embarrassed silence. 'It is the duke's land here, you say.'

'The duke invited him, sir, to rest here till Wednesday. The duke is at Strelsau, preparing the king's reception.'

'Then they're friends?'

'None better,' said the old lady.

But my rosy damsel tossed her head again; she was not to be repressed for long, and she broke out again:

'Ay, they love one another as men do who want the same place and the same wife!'

The old woman glowered; but the last words pricked my curiosity, and I interposed before she could begin scolding:

'What, the same wife, too! How's that, young lady?'

'All the world knows that Black Michael—well then, mother, the duke—would give his soul to marry his cousin, the Princess Flavia,* and that she is to be the queen.'

'Upon my word,' said I, 'I begin to be sorry for your duke. But if a man will be a younger son, why he must take what the elder leaves, and be as thankful to God as he can;' and, thinking of myself, I shrugged my shoulders and laughed. And then I thought also of Antoinette de Mauban and her journey to Strelsau.

'It's little dealing Black Michael has with——' began the girl, braving her mother's anger; but as she spoke a heavy step sounded on the floor, and a gruff voice asked in a threatening tone:

'Who talks of "Black Michael" in his Highness's own burgh?'

The girl gave a little shriek, half of fright—half, I think, of amusement.

'You'll not tell of me, Johann?' she said.

'See where your chatter leads,' said the old lady.

The man who had spoken came forward.

'We have company, Johann,' said my hostess, and the fellow plucked off his cap. A moment later he saw me, and, to my amazement, he started back a step, as though he had seen something wonderful.

'What ails you, Johann?' asked the elder girl. 'This is a gentleman on his travels, come to see the coronation.'

The man had recovered himself, but he was staring at me with an intense, searching, almost fierce glance.

'Good evening to you,' said I.

'Good evening, sir,' he muttered, still scrutinising me, and the merry girl began to laugh as she called:

'See, Johann, it is the colour you love! He started to see your hair, sir. It's not the colour we see most of here in Zenda.'

'I crave your pardon, sir,' stammered the fellow, with puzzled eyes. 'I expected to see no one.'

'Give him a glass to drink my health in; and I'll bid you good-night, and thanks to you, ladies, for your courtesy and pleasant conversation.'

So speaking, I rose to my feet, and with a slight bow turned to the door. The young girl ran to light me on the way, and the man fell back to let me pass, his eyes still fixed on me. The moment I was by, he started a step forward, asking:

'Pray, sir, do you know our king?'

'I never saw him,' said I. 'I hope to do so on Wednesday.'

He said no more, but I felt his eyes following me till the door closed behind me. My saucy conductor, looking over her shoulder at me as she preceded me upstairs, said:

'There's no pleasing Master Johann for one of your colour, sir.'

'He prefers yours, may be?' I suggested.

'I meant, sir, in a man,' she answered, with a coquettish glance.

'What,' asked I, taking hold of the other side of the candlestick, 'does colour matter in a man?'

'Nay, but I love yours—it's the Elphberg red.'

'Colour in a man,' said I, 'is a matter of no more moment than that!'—and I gave her something of no value.

'God send the kitchen-door be shut!' said she.

'Amen!' said I, and left her.

In fact, however, as I now know, colour is sometimes of considerable moment to a man.

CHAPTER III

A MERRY EVENING WITH A DISTANT RELATIVE

I WAS not so unreasonable as to be prejudiced against the duke's keeper because he disliked my complexion; and if I had been, his most civil and obliging conduct (as it seemed to me to be) next morning would have disarmed me. Hearing that I was bound for Strelsau, he came to see me while I was breakfasting, and told me that a sister of his, who had married a well-to-do tradesman and lived in the capital, had invited him to occupy a room in her house. He had gladly accepted, but now found that his duties would not permit of his absence. He begged therefore that, if such humble (though, as he added, clean and comfortable) lodgings would satisfy me, I would take his place. He pledged his sister's acquiescence, and urged the inconvenience and crowding to which I should be subject in my journeys to and from Strelsau the next day. I accepted his offer without a moment's hesitation, and he went off to telegraph to his sister, while I packed up and prepared to take the next train. But I still hankered after the forest and the shooting-lodge, and when my little maid told me that I could, by walking ten miles or so through the forest, hit the railway at a roadside station, I decided to send my luggage direct to the address which Johann had given, take my walk, and follow to Strelsau myself. Johann had gone off and was not aware of the change in my plans; but, as its only effect was to delay my arrival at his sister's for a few hours, there was no reason for troubling to inform him of it. Doubtless the good lady would waste no anxiety on my account.

I took an early luncheon, and, having bidden my kind entertainers farewell, promising to return to them on my way home, I set out to climb the hill that led to the Castle, and thence to the forest of Zenda. Half-an-hour's leisurely walking brought me to the Castle. It had been a fortress in old days, and the ancient keep was still in good preservation and very imposing. Behind it stood another portion of the original castle, and behind that again, and separated from it by a deep and broad moat, which ran all round the old buildings, was a handsome modern *château*, erected by the last king, and now forming the

country residence of the Duke of Strelsau. The old and the new por-
tions were connected by a drawbridge, and this indirect mode of
access formed the only passage between the old building and the
outer world; but leading to the modern *château* there was a broad and
handsome avenue. It was an ideal residence: when 'Black Michael'
desired company, he could dwell in his *château*; if a fit of misanthropy
seized him, he had merely to cross the bridge and draw it up after him
(it ran on rollers), and nothing short of a regiment and a train of artillery could fetch him out. I went on my way, glad that poor Black
Michael, though he could not have the throne or the princess, had, at
least, as fine a residence as any prince in Europe.

Soon I entered the forest, and walked on for an hour or more in its
cool sombre shade. The great trees enlaced with one another over my
head, and the sunshine stole through in patches as bright as diamonds, and hardly bigger. I was enchanted with the place, and, finding a felled tree-trunk, propped my back against it, and stretching my
legs out gave myself up to undisturbed contemplation of the solemn
beauty of the woods and to the comfort of a good cigar. And when the
cigar was finished and I had (I suppose) inhaled as much beauty as
I could, I went off into the most delightful sleep, regardless of my
train to Strelsau and of the fast-waning afternoon. To remember
a train in such a spot would have been rank sacrilege. Instead of that,
I fell to dreaming that I was married to the Princess Flavia and dwelt
in the Castle of Zenda, and beguiled whole days with my love in the
glades of the forest—which made a very pleasant dream. In fact,
I was just impressing a fervent kiss on the charming lips of the princess, when I heard (and the voice seemed at first a part of the dream)
someone exclaim, in rough strident tones:

'Why, the devil's in it! Shave him, and he'd be the king!'

The idea seemed whimsical enough for a dream: by the sacrifice of
my heavy moustache and carefully pointed imperial,* I was to be
transformed into a monarch! I was about to kiss the princess again,
when I arrived (very reluctantly) at the conclusion that I was awake.

I opened my eyes, and found two men regarding me with much
curiosity. Both wore shooting costumes and carried guns. One was
rather short and very stoutly built, with a big bullet-shaped head, and
bristly grey moustache, and small pale-blue eyes, a trifle bloodshot.

The other was a slender young fellow, of middle height, dark in complexion, and bearing himself with grace and distinction. I set the one down as an old soldier; the other for a gentleman accustomed to move in good society, but not unused to military life either. It turned out afterwards that my guess was a good one.

The elder man approached me, beckoning the younger to follow. He did so, courteously raising his hat. I rose slowly to my feet.

'He's the height, too!' I heard the elder murmur, as he surveyed my six feet two inches of stature. Then, with a cavalier touch of the cap, he addressed me:

'May I ask your name?'

'As you have taken the first step in the acquaintance, gentlemen,' said I, with a smile, 'suppose you give me a lead in the matter of names.'

The young man stepped forward with a pleasant smile.

'This,' said he, 'is Colonel Sapt, and I am called Fritz von Tarlenheim: we are both in the service of the King of Ruritania.'

I bowed and, baring my head, answered:

'I am Rudolf Rassendyll. I am a traveller from England; and once for a year or two I held a commission from Her Majesty the Queen.'

'Then we are all brethren of the sword,' answered Tarlenheim, holding out his hand, which I took readily.

'Rassendyll, Rassendyll!' muttered Colonel Sapt; then a gleam of intelligence flitted across his face.

'By Heaven!' he cried, 'you're of the Burlesdons?'

'My brother is now Lord Burlesdon,' said I.

'Thy head bewrayeth thee,' he chuckled, pointing to my uncovered poll.— 'Why, Fritz, you know the story?'

The young man glanced apologetically at me. He felt a delicacy which my sister-in-law would have admired. To put him at his ease, I remarked, with a smile:

'Ah! the story is known here as well as among us, it seems.'

'Known!' cried Sapt. 'If you stay here, the deuce a man in all Ruritania will doubt of it—or a woman either.'

I began to feel uncomfortable. Had I realised what a very plainly-written pedigree I carried about with me, I should have thought long before I visited Ruritania. However, I was in for it now.

At this moment a ringing voice sounded from the wood behind us:
'Fritz, Fritz! where are you, man?'

Tarlenheim started, and said hastily:

'It's the king!'

Old Sapt chuckled again.

Then a young man jumped out from behind the trunk of a tree and stood beside us. As I looked on him, I uttered an astonished cry; and he, seeing me, drew back in sudden wonder. Saving the hair on my face and a manner of conscious dignity which his position gave him, saving also that he lacked perhaps half-an-inch—nay, less than that, but still something—of my height, the King of Ruritania might have been Rudolf Rassendyll, and I, Rudolf, the King.

For an instant we stood motionless, looking at one another. Then I bared my head again and bowed respectfully. The king found his voice, and asked in bewilderment:

'Colonel—Fritz—who is this gentleman?'

I was about to answer, when Colonel Sapt stepped between the king and me, and began to talk to his Majesty in a low growl. The king towered over Sapt, and, as he listened, his eyes now and again sought mine. I looked at him long and carefully. The likeness was certainly astonishing, though I saw the points of difference also. The king's face was slightly more fleshy than mine, the oval of its contour the least trifle more pronounced, and, as I fancied, his mouth lacking something of the firmness (or obstinacy) which was to be gathered from my close-shutting lips. But, for all that, and above all minor distinctions, the likeness rose striking, salient, wonderful.

Sapt ceased speaking, and the king still frowned. Then, gradually, the corners of his mouth began to twitch, his nose came down (as mine does when I laugh), his eyes twinkled, and, behold! he burst into the merriest fit of irrepressible laughter, which rang through the woods and proclaimed him a jovial soul.

'Well met, cousin!' he cried, stepping up to me, clapping me on the back, and laughing still. 'You must forgive me if I was taken aback. A man doesn't expect to see double at this time of day, eh, Fritz?'

'I must pray pardon, sire, for my presumption,' said I. 'I trust it will not forfeit your Majesty's favour.'

'By Heaven! you'll always enjoy the king's countenance,' he laughed, 'whether I like it or not; and, sir, I shall very gladly add to it what services I can. Where are you travelling to?'

'To Strelsau, sire,—to the coronation.'

The king looked at his friends: he still smiled, though his expression hinted some uneasiness. But the humorous side of the matter caught him again.

'Fritz, Fritz!' he cried, 'a thousand crowns for a sight of brother Michael's face when he sees a pair of us!' and the merry laugh rang out again.

'Seriously,' observed Fritz von Tarlenheim, 'I question Mr. Rassendyll's wisdom in visiting Strelsau just now.'

The king lit a cigarette.

'Well, Sapt?' said he, questioningly.

'He mustn't go,' growled the old fellow.

'Come, colonel, you mean that I should be in Mr. Rassendyll's debt, if——'

'Oh, ay! wrap it up in the right way,' said Sapt, hauling a great pipe out of his pocket.

'Enough, sire,' said I. 'I'll leave Ruritania today.'

'Now, by thunder, you shan't—and that's *sans phrase*,* as Sapt likes it. For you shall dine with me tonight, happen what will afterwards. Come, man, you don't meet a new relation every day!'

'We dine sparingly tonight,' said Fritz von Tarlenheim.

'Not we—with our new cousin for a guest!' cried the king; and, as Fritz shrugged his shoulders, he added: 'Oh! I'll remember our early start, Fritz.'

'So will I—tomorrow morning,' said old Sapt, pulling at his pipe.

'O wise old Sapt!' cried the king. 'Come, Mr. Rassendyll—by the way, what name did they give you?'

'Your Majesty's,' I answered, bowing.

'Well, that shows they weren't ashamed of us,' he laughed. 'Come, then, cousin Rudolf; I've got no house of my own here, but my dear brother Michael lends us a place of his, and we'll make shift to entertain you there;' and he put his arm through mine and, signing to the others to accompany us, walked me off, westerly, through the forest.

We walked for more than half-an-hour, and the king smoked cigarettes and chattered incessantly. He was full of interest in my family, laughed heartily when I told him of the portraits with Elphberg hair in our galleries, and yet more heartily when he heard that my expedition to Ruritania was a secret one.

'You have to visit your disreputable cousin on the sly, have you?' said he.

Suddenly emerging from the wood, we came on a small and rude shooting-lodge. It was a one-story building, a sort of bungalow, built entirely of wood. As we approached it, a little man in a plain livery came out to meet us. The only other person I saw about the place was a fat elderly woman, whom I afterwards discovered to be the mother of Johann, the duke's keeper.

'Well, is dinner ready, Josef?' asked the king.

The little servant informed us that it was, and we soon sat down to a plentiful meal. The fare was plain enough: the king ate heartily, Fritz von Tarlenheim delicately, old Sapt voraciously. I played a good knife and fork, as my custom is; the king noticed my performance with approval.

'We're all good trenchermen, we Elphbergs,' said he. 'But what?—we're eating dry! Wine, Josef! wine, man! Are we beasts, to eat without drinking? Are we cattle, Josef?'

At this reproof Josef hastened to load the table with bottles.

'Remember tomorrow!' said Fritz.

'Ay—tomorrow!' said old Sapt.

The king drained a bumper to his 'Cousin Rudolf', as he was gracious—or merry—enough to call me; and I drank its fellow to the 'Elphberg Red', whereat he laughed loudly.

Now, be the meat what it might, the wine we drank was beyond all price or praise, and we did it justice. Fritz ventured once to stay the king's hand.

'What?' cried the king. 'Remember you start before I do, Master Fritz—you must be more sparing by two hours than I.'

Fritz saw that I did not understand.

'The colonel and I', he explained, 'leave here at six: we ride down to Zenda and return with the guard of honour to fetch the king at eight, and then we all ride together to the station.'

'Hang that same guard!' growled Sapt.

'Oh! it's very civil of my brother to ask the honour for his regiment,' said the king. 'Come, cousin, you need not start early. Another bottle, man!'

I had another bottle—or, rather a part of one, for the larger half travelled quickly down his Majesty's throat. Fritz gave up his attempts at persuasion: from persuading, he fell to being persuaded, and soon we were all of us as full of wine as we had any right to be. The king began talking of what he would do in the future, old Sapt of what he had done in the past, Fritz of some beautiful girl or other, and I of the wonderful merits of the Elphberg dynasty. We all talked at once, and followed to the letter Sapt's exhortation to let the morrow take care of itself.

At last the king set down his glass and leant back in his chair.

'I have drunk enough,' said he.

'Far be it from me to contradict the king,' said I.

Indeed, his remark was most absolutely true—so far as it went.

While I yet spoke, Josef came and set before the king a marvellous old wicker-covered flagon. It had lain so long in some darkened cellar that it seemed to blink in the candlelight.

'His Highness the Duke of Strelsau bade me set this wine before the king, when the king was weary of all other wines, and pray the king to drink, for the love that he bears his brother.'

'Well done, Black Michael!' said the king. 'Out with the cork, Josef. Hang him! Did he think I'd flinch from his bottle?'

The bottle was opened, and Josef filled the king's glass. The king tasted it. Then, with a solemnity born of the hour and his own condition, he looked round on us:

'Gentlemen, my friends—Rudolf, my cousin ('tis a scandalous story, Rudolf, on my honour!) everything is yours to the half of Ruritania. But ask me not for a single drop of this divine bottle, which I will drink to the health of that—that sly knave, my brother, Black Michael.'

And the king seized the bottle and turned it over his mouth, and drained it and flung it from him, and laid his head on his arms on the table.

And we drank pleasant dreams to his Majesty—and that is all I remember of the evening. Perhaps it is enough.

CHAPTER IV

THE KING KEEPS HIS APPOINTMENT

WHETHER I had slept a minute or a year I knew not. I awoke with a start and a shiver; my face, hair, and clothes dripped water, and opposite me stood old Sapt, a sneering smile on his face and an empty bucket in his hand. On the table by him sat Fritz von Tarlenheim, pale as a ghost and black as a crow under the eyes.

I leapt to my feet in anger.

'Your joke goes too far, sir!' I cried.

'Tut, man, we've no time for quarrelling. Nothing else would rouse you. It's five o'clock.'

'I'll thank you, Colonel Sapt——' I began again, hot in spirit, though I was uncommonly cold in body.

'Rassendyll,' interrupted Fritz, getting down from the table and taking my arm, 'look here.'

The king lay full length on the floor. His face was red as his hair, and he breathed heavily. Sapt, the disrespectful old dog, kicked him sharply. He did not stir, nor was there any break in his breathing. I saw that his face and head were wet with water, as were mine.

'We've spent half-an-hour on him,' said Fritz.

'He drank three times what either of you did,' growled Sapt.

I knelt down and felt his pulse. It was alarmingly languid and slow. We three looked at one another.

'Was it drugged—that last bottle?' I asked in a whisper.

'I don't know,' said Sapt.

'We must get a doctor.'

'There's none within ten miles, and a thousand doctors wouldn't take him to Strelsau today. I know the look of it. He'll not move for six or seven hours yet.'

'But the coronation!' I cried in horror.

Fritz shrugged his shoulders, as I began to see was his habit on most occasions.

'We must send word that he's ill,' he said.

'I suppose so,' said I.

Old Sapt, who seemed as fresh as a daisy, had lit his pipe and was puffing hard at it.

'If he's not crowned today,' said he, 'I'll lay a crown he's never crowned.'

'But, heavens, why?'

'The whole nation's there to meet him; half the army—ay, and Black Michael at the head. Shall we send word that the king's drunk?'

'That he's ill,' said I, in correction.

'Ill!' echoed Sapt, with a scornful laugh. 'They know his illnesses too well. He's been "ill" before!'

'Well, we must chance what they think,' said Fritz helplessly. 'I'll carry the news and make the best of it.'

Sapt raised his hand.

'Tell me,' said he. 'Do you think the king was drugged?'

'I do,' said I.

'And who drugged him?'

'That damned hound, Black Michael,' said Fritz between his teeth.

'Ay,' said Sapt, 'that he might not come to be crowned. Rassendyll here doesn't know our pretty Michael. What think you, Fritz, has Michael no king ready? Has half Strelsau no other candidate? As God's alive, man, the throne's lost if the king show himself not in Strelsau today. I know Black Michael.'

'We could carry him there,' said I.

'And a very pretty picture he makes,' sneered Sapt.

Fritz von Tarlenheim buried his face in his hands. The king breathed loudly and heavily. Sapt stirred him again with his foot.

'The drunken dog!' he said; 'but he's an Elphberg and the son of his father, and may I rot in hell before Black Michael sits in his place!'

For a moment or two we were all silent; then Sapt, knitting his bushy grey brows, took his pipe from his mouth and said to me:

'As a man grows old he believes in Fate. Fate sent you here. Fate sends you now to Strelsau.'

I staggered back, murmuring 'Good God!'

Fritz looked up with an eager, bewildered gaze.

'Impossible!' I muttered. 'I should be known.'

'It's a risk—against a certainty,' said Sapt. 'If you shave, I'll wager you'll not be known. Are you afraid?'

'Sir!'

'Come, lad, there, there; but it's your life, you know, if you're known—and mine—and Fritz's here. But, if you don't go, I swear to you Black Michael will sit tonight on the throne, and the king lie in prison or his grave.'

'The king would never forgive it,' I stammered.

'Are we women? Who cares for his forgiveness?'

The clock ticked fifty times, and sixty and seventy times, as I stood in thought. Then I suppose a look came over my face, for old Sapt caught me by the hand, crying:

'You'll go?'

'Yes, I'll go,' said I, and I turned my eyes on the prostrate figure of the king on the floor.

'Tonight,' Sapt went on in a hasty whisper, 'we are to lodge in the Palace. The moment they leave us you and I will mount our horses—Fritz must stay there and guard the king's room—and ride here at a gallop. The king will be ready—Josef will tell him—and he must ride back with me to Strelsau, and you ride as if the devil were behind you to the frontier.'

I took it all in in a second, and nodded my head.

'There's a chance,' said Fritz, with his first sign of hopefulness.

'If I escape detection,' said I.

'If we're detected,' said Sapt, 'I'll send Black Michael down below before I go myself, so help me heaven! Sit in that chair, man.'

I obeyed him.

He darted from the room, calling 'Josef! Josef!' In three minutes he was back, and Josef with him. The latter carried a jug of hot water, soap, and razors. He was trembling as Sapt told him how the land lay, and bade him shave me.

Suddenly Fritz smote on his thigh:

'But the guard! They'll know! they'll know!'

'Pooh! We shan't wait for the guard. We'll ride to Hofbau and catch a train there. When they come, the bird'll be flown.'

'But the king?'

'The king will be in the wine-cellar. I'm going to carry him there now.'

'If they find him?'

'They won't. How should they? Josef will put them off.'

'But——'

Sapt stamped his foot.

'We're not playing,' he roared. 'My God! don't I know the risk? If they do find him, he's no worse off than if he isn't crowned today in Strelsau.'

So speaking, he flung the door open and, stooping, put forth a strength I did not dream he had, and lifted the king in his hands. And as he did so, the old woman, Johann the keeper's mother, stood in the doorway. For a moment she stood, then she turned on her heel, without a sign of surprise, and clattered down the passage.

'Has she heard?' cried Fritz.

'I'll shut her mouth!' said Sapt grimly, and he bore off the king in his arms.

For me, I sat down in an arm-chair, and as I sat there, half-dazed, Josef clipped and scraped me till my moustache and imperial were things of the past and my face was as bare as the king's. And when Fritz saw me thus he drew a long breath and exclaimed:

'By Jove, we shall do it!'

It was six o'clock now, and we had no time to lose. Sapt hurried me into the king's room, and I dressed myself in the uniform of a colonel of the Guard, finding time as I slipped on the king's boots to ask Sapt what he had done with the old woman.

'She swore she'd heard nothing,' said he; 'but to make sure I tied her legs together and put a handkerchief in her mouth and bound her hands, and locked her up in the coal-cellar, next door to the king. Josef'll look after them both later on.'

Then I burst out laughing, and even old Sapt grimly smiled.

'I fancy,' said he, 'that when Josef tells them the king is gone they'll think it is because we smelt a rat. For you may swear Black Michael doesn't expect to see him in Strelsau today.'

I put the king's helmet on my head. Old Sapt handed me the king's sword, looking at me long and carefully.

'Thank God, he shaved his beard!' he exclaimed.

'Why did he?' I asked.

'Because Princess Flavia said he grazed her cheek when he was graciously pleased to give her a cousinly kiss. Come though, we must ride.'

'Is all safe here?'

'Nothing's safe anywhere,' said Sapt, 'but we can make it no safer.'

Fritz now rejoined us in the uniform of a captain in the same regiment as that to which my dress belonged. In four minutes Sapt had arrayed himself in his uniform. Josef called that the horses were ready. We jumped on their backs and started at a rapid trot. The game had begun. What would the issue of it be?

The cool morning air cleared my head, and I was able to take in all Sapt said to me. He was wonderful. Fritz hardly spoke, riding like a man asleep, but Sapt, without another word for the king, began at once to instruct me most minutely in the history of my past life, of my family, of my tastes, pursuits, weaknesses, friends, companions, and servants. He told me the etiquette of the Ruritanian Court, promising to be constantly at my elbow to point out everybody whom I ought to know, and give me hints with what degree of favour to greet them.

'By the way,' he said, 'you're a Catholic, I suppose?'

'Not I,' I answered.

'Lord, he's a heretic!'* groaned Sapt, and forthwith he fell to a rudimentary lesson in the practices and observances of the Romish faith.

'Luckily,' said he, 'you won't be expected to know much, for the king's notoriously lax and careless about such matters. But you must be as civil as butter to the Cardinal. We hope to win him over, because he and Michael have a standing quarrel about their precedence.'

We were by now at the station. Fritz had recovered nerve enough to explain to the astonished station-master that the king had changed his plans. The train steamed up. We got into a first-class carriage, and Sapt, leaning back on the cushions went on with his lesson. I looked at my watch—the king's watch it was, of course. It was just eight.

'I wonder if they've gone to look for us,' I said.

'I hope they won't find the king,' said Fritz nervously, and this time it was Sapt who shrugged his shoulders.

The train travelled well, and at half-past nine, looking out of the window, I saw the towers and spires of a great city.

'Your capital, my liege,' grinned old Sapt, with a wave of his hand, and, leaning forward, he laid his finger on my pulse. 'A little too quick,' said he, in his grumbling tone.

'I'm not made of stone!' I exclaimed.

'You'll do,' said he, with a nod. 'We must say Fritz here has caught the ague. Drain your flask, Fritz*, for heaven's sake, boy!'

Fritz did as he was bid.

'We're an hour early,' said Sapt. 'We'll send word forward of your Majesty's arrival, for there'll be no one here to meet us yet. And meanwhile——'

'Meanwhile,' said I, 'the king'll be hanged if he doesn't have some breakfast.'

Old Sapt chuckled, and held out his hand.

'You're an Elphberg, every inch of you,' said he. Then he paused, and looking at us, said quietly, 'God send we may be alive tonight!'

'Amen!' said Fritz von Tarlenheim.

The train stopped. Fritz and Sapt leapt out, uncovered, and held the door for me. I choked down a lump that rose in my throat, settled my helmet firmly on my head, and (I'm not ashamed to say it) breathed a short prayer to God. Then I stepped on the platform of the station at Strelsau.

A moment later, all was bustle and confusion: men hurrying up, hats in hand, and hurrying off again; men conducting me to the *buffet*; men mounting and riding in hot haste to the quarters of the troops, to the Cathedral, to the residence of Duke Michael. Even as I swallowed the last drop of my cup of coffee, the bells throughout all the city broke out into a joyful peal, and the sound of a military band and of men cheering smote upon my ear.

King Rudolf the Fifth was in his good city of Strelsau! And they shouted outside:

'God save the King!'

Old Sapt's mouth wrinkled into a smile.

'God save 'em both!' he whispered. 'Courage, lad!' and I felt his hand press my knee.

CHAPTER V

THE ADVENTURES OF AN UNDERSTUDY

With Fritz von Tarlenheim and Colonel Sapt close behind me, I stepped out of the *buffet* on to the platform. The last thing I did was to feel if my revolver were handy and my sword loose in the scabbard. A gay group of officers and high dignitaries stood waiting me, at their head a tall old man, covered with medals, and of military bearing. He wore the yellow-and-red ribbon of the Red Rose of Ruritania—which, by the way, decorated my unworthy breast also.

'Marshal Strakencz,' whispered Sapt, and I knew that I was in the presence of the most famous veteran of the Ruritanian army.

Just behind the Marshal stood a short, spare man, in flowing robes of black and crimson.

'The Chancellor of the Kingdom,' whispered Sapt.

The Marshal greeted me in a few loyal words, and proceeded to deliver an apology from the Duke of Strelsau. The duke, it seemed, had been afflicted with a sudden indisposition which made it impossible for him to come to the station, but he craved leave to await his Majesty at the Cathedral. I expressed my concern, accepted the Marshal's excuses very suavely, and received the compliments of a large number of distinguished personages. No one betrayed the least suspicion, and I felt my nerve returning and the agitated beating of my heart subsiding. But Fritz was still pale, and his hand shook like a leaf as he extended it to the Marshal.

Presently we formed procession and took our way to the door of the station. Here I mounted my horse, the Marshal holding my stirrup. The civil dignitaries went off to their carriages, and I started to ride through the streets with the Marshal on my right and Sapt (who, as my chief *aide-de-camp*,* was entitled to the place) on my left. The city of Strelsau is partly old and partly new. Spacious modern boulevards and residential quarters surround and embrace the narrow, tortuous and picturesque streets of the original town. In the outer circles the upper classes live; in the inner the shops are situated; and, behind their prosperous fronts, lie hidden populous but wretched lanes and

alleys, filled with a poverty-stricken, turbulent, and (in large measure) criminal class. These social and local divisions corresponded, as
I knew from Sapt's information, to another division more important
to me. The New Town was for the king; but to the Old Town Michael
of Strelsau was a hope, a hero, and a darling.

The scene was very brilliant as we passed along the Grand
Boulevard and on to the great square where the Royal Palace stood.
Here I was in the midst of my devoted adherents. Every house was
hung with red and bedecked with flags and mottoes. The streets were
lined with raised seats on each side, and I passed along, bowing this
way and that, under a shower of cheers, blessings, and waving handkerchiefs. The balconies were full of gaily dressed ladies, who clapped
their hands and curtsied and threw their brightest glances at me.
A torrent of red roses fell on me; one bloom lodged in my horse's
mane, and I took it and stuck it in my coat. The Marshal smiled
grimly. I had stolen some glances at his face, but he was too impassive
to show me whether his sympathies were with me or not.

'The red rose for the Elphbergs, Marshal,' said I gaily, and he nodded.

I have written 'gaily,' and a strange word it must seem. But the
truth is, that I was drunk with excitement. At that moment
I believed—I almost believed—that I was in very truth the king; and,
with a look of laughing triumph, I raised my eyes to the beauty-laden
balconies again ... and then I started. For, looking down on me, with
her handsome face and proud smile, was the lady who had been my
fellow-traveller—Antoinette de Mauban; and I saw her also start,
and her lips moved, and she leant forward and gazed at me. And
I, collecting myself, met her eyes full and square, while again I felt my
revolver. Suppose she had cried aloud, 'That's not the king!'

Well, we went by; and then the Marshal, turning round in his saddle, waved his hand, and the Cuirassiers* closed round us, so that the
crowd could not come near me. We were leaving my quarter and
entering Duke Michael's, and this action of the Marshal's showed me
more clearly than words what the state of feeling in the town must be.
But if Fate made me a king, the least I could do was to play the part
handsomely.

'Why this change in our order, Marshal?' said I.

The Marshal bit his white moustache.

'It is more prudent, sire,' he murmured.

I drew rein.

'Let those in front ride on,' said I, 'till they are fifty yards ahead. But do you, Marshal, and Colonel Sapt and my friends, wait here till I have ridden fifty yards. And see that no one is nearer to me. I will have my people see that their king trusts them.'

Sapt laid his hand on my arm. I shook him off. The Marshal hesitated.

'Am I not understood?' said I; and, biting his moustache again, he gave the orders. I saw old Sapt smiling into his beard, but he shook his head at me. If I had been killed in open day in the streets of Strelsau, Sapt's position would have been a difficult one.

Perhaps I ought to say that I was dressed all in white, except my boots. I wore a silver helmet with gilt ornaments, and the broad ribbon of the Rose looked well across my chest. I should be paying a poor compliment to the king if I did not set modesty aside and admit that I made a very fine figure. So the people thought; for when I, riding alone, entered the dingy, sparsely decorated, sombre streets of the Old Town, there was first a murmur, then a cheer, and a woman, from a window above a cookshop, cried the old local saying:

'If he's red, he's right!' whereat I laughed and took off my helmet that she might see that I was of the right colour, and they cheered me again at that.

It was more interesting riding thus alone, for I heard the comments of the crowd.

'He looks paler than his wont,' said one.

'You'd look pale if you lived as he does,' was the highly disrespectful retort.

'He's a bigger man than I thought,' said another.

'So he had a good jaw under that beard after all,' commented a third.

'The pictures of him aren't handsome enough,' declared a pretty girl, taking great care that I should hear. No doubt it was mere flattery.

But, in spite of these signs of approval and interest, the mass of the people received me in silence and with sullen looks, and my dear brother's portrait ornamented most of the windows—which was an ironical sort of greeting to the king. I was quite glad that he had been

spared the unpleasant sight. He was a man of quick temper, and perhaps he would not have taken it so placidly as I did.

At last we were at the Cathedral. Its great grey front, embellished
with hundreds of statues and boasting a pair of the finest oak doors in
Europe, rose for the first time before me, and the sudden sense of my
audacity almost overcame me. Everything was in a mist as I dismounted. I saw the Marshal and Sapt dimly, and dimly the throng of
gorgeously robed priests who awaited me. And my eyes were still dim
as I walked up the great nave, with the pealing of the organ in my ears.
I saw nothing of the brilliant throng that filled it, I hardly distinguished the stately figure of the Cardinal as he rose from the
archiepiscopal throne* to greet me. Two faces only stood out side by
side clearly before my eyes—the face of a girl, pale and lovely, surmounted by a crown of the glorious Elphberg hair (for in a woman it
is glorious), and the face of a man, whose full-blooded red cheeks,
black hair, and dark deep eyes told me that at last I was in presence of
my brother, Black Michael. And when he saw me his red cheeks went
pale all in a moment, and his helmet fell with a clatter on the floor.
Till that moment, I believe that he had not realised that the king was
in very truth come to Strelsau.

Of what followed next I remember nothing. I knelt before the altar
and the Cardinal anointed my head. Then I rose to my feet, and
stretched out my hand and took from him the crown of Ruritania and
set it on my head, and I swore the old oath of the king; and (if it were
a sin, may it be forgiven me) I received the Holy Sacrament there
before them all. Then the great organ pealed out again, the Marshal
bade the heralds proclaim me, and Rudolf the Fifth was crowned
king; of which imposing ceremony an excellent picture hangs now in
my dining-room. The portrait of the king is very good.

Then the lady with the pale face and the glorious hair, her train
held by two pages, stepped from her place and came to where I stood.
And a herald cried:

'Her Royal Highness the Princess Flavia!'

She curtsied low, and put her hand under mine and raised my hand
and kissed it. And for an instant I thought what I had best do. Then
I drew her to me and kissed her twice on the cheek, and she blushed
red, and—why, then his Eminence the Cardinal Archbishop slipped

in front of Black Michael, and kissed my hand and presented me with a letter from the Pope—the first and last which I have ever received from that exalted quarter!

And then came the Duke of Strelsau. His step trembled, I swear, and he looked to the right and to the left, as a man looks who thinks on flight; and his face was patched with red and white, and his hand shook so that it jumped under mine, and I felt his lips dry and parched. And I glanced at Sapt, who was smiling again into his beard, and, resolutely doing my duty in that station of life to which I had been marvellously called, I took my dear Michael by both hands and kissed him on the cheek. I think we were both glad when that was over!

But neither in the face of the princess nor in that of any other did I see the least doubt or questioning. Yet, had I and the king stood side by side, she could have told us in an instant, or, at least, on a little consideration. But neither she nor anyone else dreamed or imagined that I could be other than the king. So the likeness served, and for an hour I stood there, feeling as weary and *blasé* as though I had been a king all my life; and everybody kissed my hand, and the ambassadors paid me their respects, among them old Lord Topham, at whose house in Grosvenor Square I had danced a score of times. Thank heaven, the old man was as blind as a bat, and did not claim my acquaintance.

Then back we went through the streets to the Palace, and I heard them cheering Black Michael; but he, Fritz told me, sat biting his nails like a man in a reverie, and even his own friends said that he should have made a braver show. I was in a carriage now, side by side with the Princess Flavia, and a rough fellow cried out:

'And when's the wedding?' and as he spoke another struck him in the face, crying 'Long live Duke Michael!' and the princess coloured—it was an admirable tint—and looked straight in front of her.

Now I felt in a difficulty, because I had forgotten to ask Sapt the state of my affections, or how far matters had gone between the princess and myself. Frankly, had I been the king, the further they had gone the better should I have been pleased. For I am not a slow-blooded man, and I had not kissed Princess Flavia's cheek for nothing. These thoughts passed through my head, but, not being sure of my ground, I said nothing; and in a moment or two the princess, recovering her equanimity, turned to me.

'Do you know, Rudolf,' said she, 'you look somehow different today?'

The fact was not surprising, but the remark was disquieting.

'You look,' she went on, 'more sober, more sedate; you're almost careworn, and I declare you're thinner. Surely it's not possible that you've begun to take anything seriously?'

The princess seemed to hold of the king much the same opinion that Lady Burlesdon held of me.

I braced myself up to the conversation.

'Would that please you?' I asked softly.

'Oh, you know my views,' said she, turning her eyes away.

'Whatever pleases you I try to do,' I said; and, as I saw her smile and blush, I thought that I was playing the king's hand very well for him. So I continued, and what I said was perfectly true:

'I assure you, my dear cousin, that nothing in my life has affected me more than the reception I've been greeted with today.'

She smiled brightly, but in an instant grew grave again, and whispered:

'Did you notice Michael?'

'Yes,' said I, adding, 'He wasn't enjoying himself.'

'Do be careful!' she went on. 'You don't—indeed you don't—keep enough watch on him. You know——'

'I know,' said I, 'that he wants what I've got.'

'Yes. Hush!'

Then—and I can't justify it, for I committed the king far beyond what I had a right to do—I suppose she carried me off my feet—I went on:

'And perhaps also something which I haven't got yet, but hope to win some day.'

This was my answer. Had I been the king, I should have thought it encouraging:

'Haven't you enough responsibilities on you for one day, cousin?'

Bang, bang! Blare, blare! We were at the Palace. Guns were firing and trumpets blowing. Rows of lackeys stood waiting, and, handing the princess up the broad marble staircase, I took formal possession, as a crowned king, of the House of my ancestors, and sat down at my own table, with my cousin on my right hand, on her other side Black Michael, and on my left his Eminence the Cardinal. Behind my chair stood Sapt; and at the end of the table, I saw Fritz von Tarlenheim drain to the bottom his glass of champagne rather sooner than he decently should.

I wondered what the King of Ruritania was doing.

CHAPTER VI

THE SECRET OF A CELLAR

WE were in the king's dressing-room—Fritz von Tarlenheim, Sapt, and I. I flung myself exhausted into an armchair. Sapt lit his pipe. He uttered no congratulations on the marvellous success of our wild risk, but his whole bearing was eloquent of satisfaction. The triumph, aided perhaps by good wine, had made a new man of Fritz.

'What a day for you to remember!' he cried. 'Gad, I'd like to be a king for twelve hours myself! But, Rassendyll, you mustn't throw your heart too much into the part. I don't wonder Black Michael looked blacker than ever—you and the princess had so much to say to one another.'

'How beautiful she is!' I exclaimed.

'Never mind the women,' growled Sapt. 'Are you ready to start?'

'Yes,' said I, with a sigh.

It was five o'clock, and at twelve I should be no more than Rudolf Rassendyll. I remarked on it in a joking tone.

'You'll be lucky,' observed Sapt grimly, 'if you're not the late Rudolf Rassendyll. By Heaven! I feel my head wobbling on my shoulders every minute you're in the city. Do you know, friend, that Michael has had news from Zenda? He went into a room alone to read it—and he came out looking like a man dazed.'

'I'm ready,' said I, this news making me none the more eager to linger.

Sapt sat down.

'I must write us an order to leave the city. Michael's Governor, you know, and we must be prepared for hindrances. You must sign the order.'

'My dear colonel, I've not been bred a forger!'

Out of his pocket Sapt produced a piece of paper.

'There's the king's signature,' he said, 'and here,' he went on, after another search in his pocket, 'is some tracing paper. If you can't manage a "Rudolf" in ten minutes, why—I can.'

'Your education has been more comprehensive than mine,' said I. 'You write it.'

And a very tolerable forgery did this versatile hero produce.

'Now Fritz,' said he, 'the king goes to bed. He is upset. No one is here to see him till nine o'clock tomorrow. You understand—no one?'

'I understand,' answered Fritz.

'Michael may come, and claim immediate audience. You'll answer that only princes of the blood* are entitled to it.'

'That'll annoy Michael,' laughed Fritz.

'You quite understand?' asked Sapt again. 'If the door of this room is opened while we're away, you're not to be alive to tell us about it.'

'I need no schooling, colonel,' said Fritz, a trifle haughtily.

'Here, wrap yourself in this big cloak,' Sapt continued to me, 'and put on this flat cap. My orderly rides with me to the shooting-lodge tonight.'

'There's an obstacle,' I observed. 'The horse doesn't live that can carry me forty miles.'

'Oh, yes, he does—two of him: one here—one at the lodge. Now, are you ready?'

'I'm ready,' said I.

Fritz held out his hand.

'In case,' said he; and we shook hands heartily.

'Damn your sentiment!' growled Sapt. 'Come along.'

He went, not to the door, but to a panel in the wall.

'In the old king's time,' said he, 'I knew this way well.'

I followed him, and we walked, as I should estimate, near two hundred yards along a narrow passage. Then we came to a stout oak door. Sapt unlocked it. We passed through, and found ourselves in a quiet street that ran along the back of the Palace gardens. A man was waiting for us with two horses. One was a magnificent bay, up to any weight; the other a sturdy brown. Sapt signed to me to mount the bay. Without a word to the man, we mounted and rode away. The town was full of noise and merriment, but we took secluded ways. My cloak was wrapped over half my face; the capacious flat cap hid every lock of my tell-tale hair. By Sapt's directions, I crouched on my saddle, and rode with such a round back as I hope never to exhibit on a horse again. Down a long narrow lane we went, meeting some wanderers and some roisterers; and, as we rode, we heard the Cathedral bells still clanging out their welcome to the king. It was half-past six, and still light. At last we came to the city wall and to a gate.

'Have your weapon ready,' whispered Sapt. 'We must stop his mouth, if he talks.'

I put my hand on my revolver. Sapt hailed the door-keeper. The stars fought for us! A little girl of fourteen tripped out.

'Please, sir, father's gone to see the king.'

'He'd better have stayed here,' said Sapt to me, grinning.

'But he said I wasn't to open the gate, sir.'

'Did he, my dear?' said Sapt, dismounting. 'Then give me the key.'

The key was in the child's hand. Sapt gave her a crown.

'Here's an order from the king. Show it to your father. Orderly, open the gate!'

I leapt down. Between us we rolled back the great gate, led our horses out, and closed it again.

'I shall be sorry for the doorkeeper, if Michael finds out that he wasn't there. Now then, lad, for a canter. We mustn't go too fast while we're near the town.'

Once, however, outside the city, we ran little danger, for everybody else was inside, merry-making; and as the evening fell we quickened our pace, my splendid horse bounding along under me as though I had been a feather. It was a fine night, and presently the moon appeared. We talked little on the way, and chiefly about the progress we were making.

'I wonder what the duke's despatches told him!' said I, once.

'Ah, I wonder!' responded Sapt.

We stopped for a draught of wine and to bait our horses, losing half-an-hour thus. I dared not go into the inn, and stayed with the horses in the stable. Then we went ahead again, and had covered some five-and-twenty miles, when Sapt abruptly stopped.

'Hark!' he cried.

I listened. Away, far behind us, in the still of the evening—it was just half-past nine—we heard the beat of horses' hoofs. The wind blowing strong behind us, carried the sound. I glanced at Sapt.

'Come on!' he cried, and spurred his horse into a gallop. When we next paused to listen, the hoof-beats were not audible, and we relaxed our pace. Then we heard them again. Sapt jumped down and laid his ear to the ground.

'There are two,' he said. 'They're only a mile behind. Thank God the road curves in and out, and the wind's our way.'

We galloped on. We seemed to be holding our own. We had entered the outskirts of the forest of Zenda, and the trees, closing in behind us as the track zigged and zagged, prevented us seeing our pursuers, and them from seeing us.

Another half-hour brought us to a divide of the road. Sapt drew rein.

'To the right is our road,' he said. 'To the left, to the Castle. Each about eight miles. Get down.'

'But they'll be on us!' I cried.

'Get down!' he repeated, brusquely; and I obeyed.

The wood was dense up to the very edge of the road. We led our horses into the covert, bound handkerchiefs over their eyes, and stood beside them.

'You want to see who they are?' I whispered.

'Ay, and where they're going,' he answered.

I saw that his revolver was in his hand.

Nearer and nearer came the hoofs. The moon shone out now clear and full, so that the road was white with it. The ground was hard, and we had left no traces.

'Here they come!' whispered Sapt.

'It's the duke!'

'I thought so!' he answered.

It was the duke; and with him a burly fellow whom I knew well, and who had cause to know me afterwards—Max Holf,* brother to Johann the keeper, and body-servant to his Highness. They were up to us: the duke reined up. I saw Sapt's finger curl lovingly towards the trigger. I believe he would have given ten years of his life for a shot; and he could have picked off Black Michael as easily as I could a barn-door fowl in a farmyard. I laid my hand on his arm. He nodded reassuringly: he was always ready to sacrifice inclination to duty.

'Which way?' asked Black Michael.

'To the Castle, your Highness,' urged his companion. 'There we shall learn the truth.'

For an instant the duke hesitated.

'I thought I heard hoofs,' said he.

'I think not, your Highness.'

'Why shouldn't we go to the lodge?'

'I fear a trap. If all is well, why go to the lodge? If not, it's a snare to trap us.'

Suddenly the duke's horse neighed. In an instant we folded our cloaks close round our horses' heads, and, holding them thus, covered the duke and his attendant with our revolvers. If they had found us, they had been dead men, or our prisoners.

Michael waited a moment longer. Then he cried:

'To Zenda, then!' and setting spurs to his horse, galloped on.

Sapt raised his weapon after him, and there was such an expression of wistful regret on his face that I had much ado not to burst out laughing.

For ten minutes we stayed where we were.

'You see,' said Sapt, 'they've sent him news that all is well.'

'What does that mean?' I asked.

'God knows,' said Sapt, frowning heavily. 'But it's brought him from Strelsau in a rare puzzle.'

Then we mounted, and rode fast as our weary horses could lay their feet to the ground. For those last eight miles we spoke no more. Our minds were full of apprehension. 'All is well.' What did it mean? Was all well with the king?

At last the lodge came in sight. Spurring our horses to a last gallop, we rode up to the gate. All was still and quiet. Not a soul came to meet us. We dismounted in haste. Suddenly Sapt caught me by the arm.

'Look there!' he said, pointing to the ground.

I looked down. At my feet lay five or six silk handkerchiefs, torn and slashed and rent. I turned to him questioningly.

'They're what I tied the old woman up with,' said he. 'Fasten the horses, and come along.'

The handle of the door turned without resistance. We passed into the room which had been the scene of last night's bout. It was still strewn with the remnants of our meal and with empty bottles.

'Come on,' cried Sapt, whose marvellous composure had at last almost given way.

We rushed down the passage towards the cellars. The door of the coal-cellar stood wide open.

'They found the old woman,' said I.

'You might have known that from the handkerchiefs,' he said.

Then we came opposite the door of the wine-cellar. It was shut. It looked in all respects as it had looked when we left it that morning.

'Come, it's all right,' said I.

A loud oath from Sapt rang out. His face turned pale, and he pointed again at the floor. From under the door a red stain had spread over the floor of the passage and dried there. Sapt sank against the opposite wall. I tried the door. It was locked.

'Where's Josef?' muttered Sapt.

'Where's the king?' I responded.

Sapt took out a flask and put it to his lips. I ran back to the dining-room, and seized a heavy poker from the fire-place. In my terror and excitement I rained blows on the lock of the door, and I fired a cartridge into it. It gave way, and the door swung open.

'Give me a light,' said I; but Sapt still leant against the wall.

He was, of course, more moved than I, for he loved his master. Afraid for himself he was not—no man ever saw him that; but to think what might lie in that dark cellar was enough to turn any man's face pale. I went myself, and took a silver candlestick from the dining-table and struck a light, and, as I returned, I felt the hot wax drip on my naked hand as the candle swayed to and fro; so that I cannot afford to despise Colonel Sapt for his agitation.

I came to the door of the cellar. The red stain, turning more and more to a dull brown, stretched inside. I walked two yards into the cellar, and held the candle high above my head. I saw the full bins of wine; I saw spiders crawling on the walls; I saw, too, a couple of empty bottles lying on the floor; and then, away in the corner, I saw the body of a man, lying flat on his back, with his arms stretched wide, and a crimson gash across his throat. I walked to him and knelt down beside him, and commended to God the soul of a faithful man. For it was the body of Josef, the little servant, slain in guarding the king.

I felt a hand on my shoulders, and, turning, saw Sapt's eyes, glaring and terror-struck, beside me.

'The king? My God! The king?' he whispered hoarsely.

I threw the candle's gleam over every inch of the cellar.

'The king is not here,' said I.

CHAPTER VII

HIS MAJESTY SLEEPS IN STRELSAU

I PUT my arm round Sapt's waist and supported him out of the cellar, drawing the battered door close after me. For ten minutes or more we sat silent in the dining-room. Then old Sapt rubbed his knuckles into his eyes, gave one great gasp, and was himself again. As the clock on the mantel-piece struck one he stamped his foot on the floor, saying:

'They've got the king!'

'Yes,' said I, '"all's well!" as Black Michael's despatch said. What a moment it must have been for him when the royal salutes fired at Strelsau this morning! I wonder when he got the message!'

'It must have been sent in the morning,' said Sapt. 'They must have sent it before news of your arrival at Strelsau reached Zenda— I suppose it came from Zenda.'

'And he's carried it about all day!' I exclaimed. 'Upon my honour, I'm not the only man who's had a trying day! What did he think, Sapt?'

'What does that matter? What does he think, lad, now?'

I rose to my feet.

'We must get back,' I said, 'and rouse every soldier in Strelsau. We ought to be in pursuit of Michael before midday.'

Old Sapt pulled out his pipe and carefully lit it from the candle which guttered on the table.

'The king may be murdered while we sit here!' I urged.

Sapt smoked on for a moment in silence.

'That cursed old woman!' he broke out. 'She must have attracted their attention somehow. I see the game. They came up to kidnap the king, and—as I say—somehow they found him. If you hadn't gone to Strelsau, you and I and Fritz had been in heaven by now!'

'And the king?'

'Who knows where the king is now?' he asked.

'Come, let's be off!' said I; but he sat still. And suddenly he burst into one of his grating chuckles:

'By Jove, we've shaken up Black Michael!'

'Come, come!' I repeated impatiently.

'And we'll shake him up a bit more,' he added, a cunning smile broadening on his wrinkled, weather-beaten face and his teeth working on an end of his grizzled moustache. 'Ay, lad, we'll go back to Strelsau. The king shall be in his capital again tomorrow.'

'The king?'

'The crowned king!'

'You're mad!' I cried.

'If we go back and tell the trick we played, what would you give for our lives?'

'Just what they're worth,' said I.

'And for the king's throne? Do you think that the nobles and the people will enjoy being fooled as you've fooled them? Do you think they'll love a king who was too drunk to be crowned, and sent a servant to personate* him?'

'He was drugged—and I'm no servant.'

'Mine will be Black Michael's version.'

He rose, came to me, and laid his hand on my shoulder.

'Lad,' he said, 'if you play the man, you may save the king yet. Go back and keep his throne warm for him.'

'But the duke knows—the villains he has employed know——'

'Ah, but they can't speak!' roared Sapt, in grim triumph. 'We've got 'em! How can they denounce you without denouncing themselves? "This is not the king, because we kidnapped the king and murdered his servant." Can they say that?'

The position flashed on me. Whether Michael knew me or not, he could not speak. Unless he produced the king, what could he do? And if he produced the king, where was he? For a moment I was carried away headlong; but in an instant the difficulties came strong upon me.

'I must be found out,' I urged.

'Perhaps; but every hour's something. Above all, we must have a king in Strelsau, or the city will be Michael's in four-and-twenty hours, and what would the king's life be worth then—or his throne? Lad, you must do it!'

'Suppose they kill the king?'

'They'll kill him, if you don't.'

'Sapt, suppose they have killed the king?'

'Then, by heaven, you're as good an Elphberg as Black Michael, and you shall reign in Ruritania! But I don't believe they have; nor will they kill him if you're on the throne. Will they kill him, to put you in?'

It was a wild plan—wilder even and more hopeless than the trick we had already carried through; but as I listened to Sapt I saw the strong points in our game. And then I was a young man and I loved action, and I was offered such a hand in such a game as perhaps never man played yet.

'I shall be found out,' I said.

'Perhaps,' said Sapt. 'Come! to Strelsau! We shall be caught like rats in a trap if we stay here.'

'Sapt,' I cried, 'I'll try it!'

'Well played!' said he. 'I hope they've left us the horses. I'll go and see.'

'We must bury that poor fellow,' said I.

'No time,' said Sapt.

'I'll do it.'

'Hang you!' he grinned. 'I make you a king, and——Well, do it. Go and fetch him, while I look to the horses. He can't lie very deep, but I doubt if he'll care about that. Poor little Josef! He was an honest bit of a man.'

He went out, and I went to the cellar. I raised poor Josef in my arms and bore him into the passage and thence towards the door of the house. Just inside I laid him down, remembering that I must find spades for our task. At this instant Sapt came up.

'The horses are all right; there's the own brother to the one that brought you here. But you may save yourself that job.'

'I'll not go before he's buried.'

'Yes, you will.'

'Not I, Colonel Sapt; not for all Ruritania.'

'You fool!' said he. 'Come here.'

He drew me to the door. The moon was sinking, but about three hundred yards away, coming along the road from Zenda, I made out a party of men. There were seven or eight of them; four were on horseback and the rest were walking, and I saw that they carried long implements, which I guessed to be spades and mattocks, on their shoulders.

'They'll save you the trouble,' said Sapt. 'Come along.'

He was right. The approaching party must, beyond doubt, be Duke Michael's men, come to remove the traces of their evil work. I hesitated no longer, but an irresistible desire seized me. Pointing to the corpse of poor little Josef, I said to Sapt:

'Colonel, we ought to strike a blow for him!'

'You'd like to give him some company, eh? But it's too risky work, your Majesty.'

'I must have a slap at 'em,' said I.

Sapt wavered.

'Well,' said he, 'it's not business, you know; but you've been a good boy—and if we come to grief, why, hang me, it'll save us a lot of thinking! I'll show you how to touch them.'

He cautiously closed the open chink of the door. Then we retreated through the house and made our way to the back entrance. Here our horses were standing. A carriage-drive swept all round the lodge.

'Revolver ready?' asked Sapt.

'No; steel for me,' said I.

'Gad, you're thirsty tonight,' chuckled Sapt. 'So be it.'

We mounted, drawing our swords, and waited silently for a minute or two. Then we heard the tramp of men on the drive the other side of the house. They came to a stand, and one cried:

'Now then, fetch him out!'

'Now!' whispered Sapt.

Driving the spurs into our horses, we rushed at a gallop round the house, and in a moment we were among the ruffians. Sapt told me afterwards that he killed a man, and I believe him; but I saw no more of him. With a cut, I split the head of a fellow on a brown horse, and he fell to the ground. Then I found myself opposite a big man, and I was half-conscious of another to my right. It was too warm to stay, and with a simultaneous action I drove my spurs into my horse again and my sword full into the big man's breast. His bullet whizzed past my ear—I could almost swear it touched it. I wrenched at the sword, but it would not come, and I dropped it and galloped after Sapt, whom I now saw about twenty yards ahead. I waved my hand in farewell, and dropped it a second later with a yell, for a bullet had grazed my finger and I felt the blood. Old Sapt turned round in the saddle. Someone fired again, but they had no rifles, and we were out of range. Sapt fell to laughing.

'That's one to me and two to you, with decent luck,' said he. 'Little Josef will have company.'

'Ay, they'll be a *partie carrée*,'* said I. My blood was up, and I rejoiced to have killed them.

'Well, a pleasant night's work to the rest!' said he. 'I wonder if they noticed you!'

'The big fellow did; as I stuck him I heard him cry, "The king!"'

'Good! good! Oh, we'll give Black Michael some work before we've done!'

Pausing an instant, we made a bandage for my wounded finger, which was bleeding freely and ached severely, the bone being much bruised. Then we rode on, asking of our good horses all that was in them. The excitement of the fight and of our great resolve died away, and we rode in gloomy silence. Day broke clear and cold. We found a farmer just up, and made him give us sustenance for ourselves and our horses. I, feigning a toothache, muffled my face closely. Then ahead again, till Strelsau lay before us. It was eight o'clock or nearing nine, and the gates were all open, as they always were save when the duke's caprice or intrigues shut them. We rode in by the same way as we had come out the evening before, all four of us—the men and the horses—wearied and jaded. The streets were even quieter than when we had gone: everyone was sleeping off last night's revelry, and we met hardly a soul till we reached the little gate of the Palace. There Sapt's old groom was waiting for us.

'Is all well, sir?' he asked.

'All's well,' said Sapt, and the man, coming to me, took my hand to kiss.

'The king's hurt!' he cried.

'It's nothing,' said I, as I dismounted; 'I caught my finger in the door.'

'Remember—silence!' said Sapt. 'Ah! but, my good Freyler, I do not need to tell you that!'

The old fellow shrugged his shoulders.

'All young men like to ride abroad now and again, why not the king?' said he; and Sapt's laugh left his opinion of my motives undisturbed.

'You should always trust a man,' observed Sapt, fitting the key in the lock,—'just as far as you must.'

We went in and reached the dressing-room. Flinging open the door, we saw Fritz von Tarlenheim stretched, fully dressed, on the sofa. He seemed to have been sleeping, but our entry woke him. He leapt to his feet, gave one glance at me, and with a joyful cry, threw himself on his knees before me.

'Thank God, sire! thank God, you're safe!' he cried, stretching his hand up to catch hold of mine.

I confess that I was moved. This king, whatever his faults, made people love him. For a moment I could not bear to speak or break the poor fellow's illusion. But tough old Sapt had no such feeling. He slapped his hand on his thigh delightedly.

'Bravo, lad!' cried he. 'We shall do!'

Fritz looked up in bewilderment. I held out my hand.

'You're wounded, sire!' he exclaimed.

'It's only a scratch,' said I, 'but——' I paused.

He rose to his feet with a bewildered air. Holding my hand, he looked up and down, and down and up. Then suddenly he dropped my hand and reeled back.

'Where's the king? Where's the king?' he cried.

'Hush, you fool!' hissed Sapt. 'Not so loud! Here's the king!'

A knock sounded at the door. Sapt seized me by the hand.

'Here, quick, to the bedroom! Off with your cap and your boots. Get into bed. Cover everything up.'

I did as I was bid. A moment later Sapt looked in, nodded, grinned, and introduced an extremely smart and deferential young gentleman, who came up to my bedside, bowing again and again, and informed me that he was of the household of the Princess Flavia, and that her Royal Highness had sent him especially to inquire how the king's health was after the fatigues which his Majesty had undergone yesterday.

'My best thanks, sir, to my cousin,' said I; 'and tell her Royal Highness that I was never better in my life.'

'The king,' added old Sapt (who, I began to find, loved a good lie for its own sake), 'has slept without a break all night.'

The young gentleman (he reminded me of 'Osric' in *Hamlet**) bowed himself out again. The farce was over, and Fritz von Tarlenheim's pale face recalled us to reality,—though, in faith, the farce had to be reality for us now.

'Is the king dead?' he whispered.

'Please God, no,' said I. 'But he's in the hands of Black Michael!'

CHAPTER VIII

A FAIR COUSIN AND A DARK BROTHER

A REAL king's life is perhaps a hard one; but a pretended king's is, I warrant, much harder. On the next day, Sapt instructed me in my duties—what I ought to do and what I ought to know—for three hours; then I snatched breakfast, with Sapt still opposite me, telling me that the king always took white wine in the morning and was known to detest all highly seasoned dishes. Then came the Chancellor, for another three hours; and to him I had to explain that the hurt to my finger (we turned that bullet to happy account) prevented me from writing—whence arose great to-do, hunting of precedents and so forth, ending in my 'making my mark',* and the Chancellor attesting it with a superfluity of solemn oaths. Then the French ambassador was introduced, to present his credentials; here my ignorance was of no importance, as the king would have been equally raw to the business (we worked through the whole *corps diplomatique** in the next few days, a demise of the Crown necessitating all this pother.

Then, at last, I was left alone. I called my new servant (we had chosen, to succeed poor Josef, a young man who had never known the king), had a brandy-and-soda brought to me, and observed to Sapt that I trusted that I might now have a rest.

Fritz von Tarlenheim was standing by.

'By Heaven!' he cried, 'we waste time. Aren't we going to throw Black Michael by the heels?'

'Gently, my son, gently,' said Sapt, knitting his brows. 'It would be a pleasure, but it might cost us dear. Would Michael fall and leave the king alive?'

'And,' I suggested, 'while the king is here in Strelsau, on his throne, what grievance has he against his dear brother Michael?'

'Are we to do nothing, then?'

'We're to do nothing stupid,' growled Sapt.

'In fact, Fritz,' said I, 'I am reminded of a situation in one of our English plays—*The Critic**—have you heard of it? Or, if you like, of two men, each covering the other with a revolver. For I can't expose Michael without exposing myself——'

'And the king,' put in Sapt.

'And, hang me if Michael won't expose himself, if he tries to expose me!'

'It's very pretty,' said old Sapt.

'If I'm found out,' I pursued, 'I will make a clean breast of it, and fight it out with the duke; but at present I'm waiting for a move from him.'

'He'll kill the king,' said Fritz.

'Not he,' said Sapt.

'Half of the Six are in Strelsau,' said Fritz.

'Only half? You're sure?' asked Sapt eagerly.

'Yes—only half.'

'Then the king's alive, for the other three are guarding him!' cried Sapt.

'Yes—you're right!' exclaimed Fritz, his face brightening. 'If the king were dead and buried, they'd all be here with Michael. You know Michael's back, colonel?'

'I know, curse him!'

'Gentlemen, gentlemen,' said I, 'who are the Six?'

'I think you'll make their acquaintance soon,' said Sapt. 'They are six gentlemen whom Michael maintains in his household: they belong to him body and soul. There are three Ruritanians; then there's a Frenchman, a Belgian, and one of your countrymen.'

'They'd all cut a throat if Michael told them,' said Fritz.

'Perhaps they'll cut mine,' I suggested.

'Nothing more likely,' agreed Sapt. 'Who are here, Fritz?'

'De Gautet, Bersonin, and Detchard.'

'The foreigners! It's as plain as a pikestaff. He's brought them, and left the Ruritanians with the king: that's because he wants to commit the Ruritanians as deep as he can.'

'They were none of them among our friends at the lodge, then?' I asked.

'I wish they had been,' said Sapt, wistfully. 'They had been, not Six, but Four, by now.'

I had already developed one attribute of royalty—a feeling that

I need not reveal all my mind or my secret designs even to my intimate friends. I had fully resolved on my course of action. I meant to make myself as popular as I could, and at the same time to show no disfavour to Michael. By these means I hoped to allay the hostility of his adherents, and make it appear, if an open conflict came about, that he was ungrateful and not oppressed.

Yet an open conflict was not what I hoped for.

The king's interest demanded secrecy; and while secrecy lasted, I had a fine game to play in Strelsau. Michael should not grow stronger for delay!

I ordered my horse, and, attended by Fritz von Tarlenheim, rode in the grand new avenue of the Royal Park, returning all the salutes which I received with punctilious politeness. Then I rode through a few of the streets, stopped and bought flowers of a pretty girl, paying her with a piece of gold; and then, having attracted the desired amount of attention (for I had a trail of half-a-thousand people after me), I rode to the residence of the Princess Flavia, and asked if she would receive me. This step created much interest, and was met with shouts of approval. The princess was very popular, and the Chancellor himself had not scrupled to hint to me that the more I pressed my suit, and the more rapidly I brought it to a prosperous conclusion, the stronger should I be in the affection of my subjects. The Chancellor, of course, did not understand the difficulties which lay in the way of following his loyal and excellent advice. However, I thought I could do no harm by calling; and in this view Fritz supported me with a cordiality that surprised me, until he confessed that he also had his motives for liking a visit to the princess's house, which motive was no other than a great desire to see the princess's lady-in-waiting and bosom friend, the Countess Helga von Strofzin.

Etiquette seconded Fritz's hopes. While I was ushered into the princess's room, he remained with the countess in the ante-chamber: in spite of the people and servants who were hanging about, I doubt not that they managed a *tête-à-tête*; but I had no leisure to think of them, for I was playing the most delicate move in all my difficult game. I had to keep the princess devoted to me—and yet indifferent to me: I had to show affection for her—and not feel it. I had to make love for another, and that to a girl who—princess or no princess—was the most beautiful I had ever seen. Well, I braced myself to the task, made no easier by the charming embarrassment with which I was received. How I succeeded in carrying out my programme will appear hereafter.

'You are gaining golden laurels,' she said. 'You are like the prince in Shakespeare who was transformed by becoming king.* But I'm forgetting you are king, sire.'

'I ask you to speak nothing but what your heart tells you—and to call me nothing but my name.'

She looked at me for a moment.

'Then I'm glad and proud, Rudolf,' said she. 'Why, as I told you, your very face is changed.'

I acknowledged the compliment, but I disliked the topic; so I said: 'My brother is back, I hear. He made an excursion, didn't he?'

'Yes, he is here,' she said, frowning a little.

'He can't stay long from Strelsau, it seems,' I observed, smiling. 'Well, we are all glad to see him. The nearer he is, the better.'

The princess glanced at me with a gleam of amusement in her eyes.

'Why, cousin? Is it that you can——?'

'See better what he's doing? Perhaps,' said I. 'And why are you glad?'

'I didn't say I was glad,' she answered.

'Some people say so for you.'

'There are many insolent people,' she said, with delightful haughtiness.

'Possibly you mean that I am one?'

'Your Majesty could not be,' she said, curtseying in feigned deference, but adding, mischievously, after a pause: 'Unless, that is——'

'Well, unless what?'

'Unless you tell me that I mind a snap of my fingers where the Duke of Strelsau is.'

Really, I wished that I had been the king.

'You don't care where cousin Michael——'

'Ah, cousin Michael! I call him the Duke of Strelsau.'

'You call him Michael when you meet him?'

'Yes—by the orders of your father.'

'I see. And now by mine?'

'If those are your orders.'

'Oh, decidedly! We must all be pleasant to our dear Michael.'

'You order me to receive his friends, too, I suppose?'

'The Six?'

'You call them that, too?'

'To be in the fashion, I do. But I order you to receive no one unless you like.'

'Except yourself?'

'I pray for myself. I could not order.'

As I spoke, there came a cheer from the street. The princess ran to the window.

'It is he!' she cried. 'It is—the Duke of Strelsau!'

I smiled, but said nothing. She returned to her seat. For a few moments we sat in silence. The noise outside subsided, but I heard the tread of feet in the ante-room. I began to talk on general subjects. This went on for some minutes. I wondered what had become of Michael, but it did not seem to be for me to interfere. All at once, to my great surprise, Flavia, clasping her hands, asked in an agitated voice:

'Are you wise to make him angry?'

'What? Who? How am I making him angry?'

'Why, by keeping him waiting.'

'My dear cousin, I don't want to keep him——'

'Well, then, is he to come in?'

'Of course, if you wish it.'

She looked at me curiously.

'How funny you are,' she said. 'Of course no one could be announced while I was with you.'

Here was a charming attribute of royalty!

'An excellent etiquette!' I cried. 'But I had clean forgotten it; and if I were alone with someone else, couldn't you be announced?'

'You know as well as I do. I could be, because I am of the Blood;'* and she still looked puzzled.

'I never could remember all these silly rules,' said I, rather feebly, as I inwardly cursed Fritz for not posting me up. 'But I'll repair my fault.'

I jumped up, flung open the door, and advanced into the ante-room. Michael was sitting at a table, a heavy frown on his face. Everyone else was standing, save that impudent young dog Fritz, who was lounging easily in an arm-chair, and flirting with the Countess Helga. He leapt up as I entered, with a deferential alacrity that lent point to his former nonchalance. I had no difficulty in understanding that the duke might not like young Fritz.

I held out my hand, Michael took it, and I embraced him. Then I drew him with me into the inner room.

'Brother,' I said, 'if I had known you were here, you should not have waited a moment before I asked the princess to permit me to bring you to her.'

He thanked me, but coldly. The man had many qualities, but he could not hide his feelings. A mere stranger could have seen that he hated me, and hated worse to see me with Princess Flavia; yet I am persuaded that he tried to conceal both feelings, and, further, that he tried to persuade me that he believed I was verily the king. I did not know, of course; but, unless the king were an impostor, at once cleverer and more audacious than I (and I began to think something of myself in that *rôle*), Michael could not believe that. And, if he didn't, how he must have loathed paying me deference, and hearing my 'Michael' and my 'Flavia'!

'Your hand is hurt, sir,' he observed, with concern.

'Yes; I was playing a game with a mongrel dog' (I meant to stir him), 'and you know, brother, such have uncertain tempers.'

He smiled sourly, and his dark eyes rested on me for a moment.

'But is there no danger from the bite?' cried Flavia, anxiously.

'None from this,' said I. 'If I gave him a chance to bite deeper, it would be different, cousin.'

'But surely he has been destroyed?' said she.

'Not yet. We're waiting to see if his bite is harmful.'

'And if it is?' asked Michael, with his sour smile.

'He'll be knocked on the head, brother,' said I.

'You won't play with him any more?' urged Flavia.

'Perhaps I shall.'

'He might bite again.'

'Doubtless he'll try,' said I, smiling.

Then, fearing Michael would say something which I must appear to resent (for, though I might show him my hate, I must seem to be full of favour), I began to compliment him on the magnificent condition of his regiment, and of their loyal greeting to me on the day of my coronation. Thence I passed to a rapturous description of the shooting-lodge which he had lent me. But he rose suddenly to his feet. His temper was failing him, and, with an excuse, he said farewell. However, as he reached the door he stopped, saying:

'Three friends of mine are very anxious to have the honour of being presented to you, sire. They are here in the ante-chamber.'

I joined him directly, passing my arm through his. The look on his face was honey to me. We entered the antechamber in fraternal fashion. Michael beckoned, and three men came forward.

'These gentlemen,' said Michael, with a stately courtesy which, to do him justice, he could assume with perfect grace and ease, 'are the loyalest and most devoted of your Majesty's servants, and are my very faithful and attached friends.'

'On the last ground as much as the first,' said I, 'I am very pleased to see them.'

They came one by one and kissed my hand—De Gautet, a tall lean fellow, with hair standing straight up and waxed moustache; Bersonin, the Belgian, a portly man of middle height with a bald head (though he was not far past thirty); and, last, the Englishman, Detchard, a narrow-faced fellow, with close-cut fair hair and a bronzed complexion. He was a finely made man, broad in the shoulders and slender in the hips. A good fighter, but a crooked customer, I put him down for. I spoke to him in English,* with a slight foreign accent, and I swear the fellow smiled, though he hid the smile in an instant.

'So Mr. Detchard is in the secret,' thought I.

Having got rid of my dear brother and his friends, I returned to make my adieu to my cousin. She was standing at the door. I bade her farewell, taking her hand in mind.

'Rudolf,' she said, very low, 'be careful, won't you?'

'Of what?'

'You know—I can't say. But think what your life is to——'

'Well, to——?'

'To Ruritania.'

Was I right to play the part, or wrong to play the part? I know not: evil lay both ways, and I dared not tell her the truth.

'Only to Ruritania?' I asked softly.

A sudden flush spread over her incomparable face.

'To your friends, too,' she said.

'Friends?'

'And to your cousin,' she whispered, 'and loving servant.'

I could not speak. I kissed her hand, and went out cursing myself.

Outside I found Master Fritz, quite reckless of the footmen, playing at cat's-cradle* with the Countess Helga.

'Hang it!' said he, 'we can't always be plotting. Love claims his share.'

'I'm inclined to think he does,' said I; and Fritz, who had been by my side, dropped respectfully behind.

CHAPTER IX

A NEW USE FOR A TEA-TABLE

I<small>F</small> I were to detail the ordinary events of my daily life at this time, they might prove instructive to people who are not familiar with the insides of palaces; if I revealed some of the secrets I learnt, they might prove of interest to the statesmen of Europe. I intend to do neither of these things. I should be between the Scylla of dulness and the Charybdis* of indiscretion, and I feel that I had far better confine myself strictly to the underground drama which was being played beneath the surface of Ruritanian politics. I need only say that the secret of my imposture defied detection. I made mistakes. I had bad minutes: it needed all the tact and graciousness whereof I was master to smooth over some apparent lapses of memory and unmindfulness of old acquaintances of which I was guilty. But I escaped, and I attribute my escape, as I have said before, most of all, to the very audacity of the enterprise. It is my belief that, given the necessary physical likeness, it was far easier to pretend to be King of Ruritania than it would have been to personate my next-door neighbour.

One day Sapt came into my room. He threw me a letter, saying:

'That's for you—a woman's hand, I think. But I've some news for you first.'

'What's that?'

'The king's at the Castle of Zenda,' said he.

'How do you know?'

'Because the other half of Michael's Six are there. I had enquiries made, and they're all there—Lauengram, Krafstein, and young Rupert Hentzau; three rogues, too, on my honour, as fine as live in Ruritania.'

'Well?'

'Well, Fritz wants you to march to the Castle with horse, foot, and artillery.'

'And drag the moat?' I asked.

'That would be about it,' grinned Sapt; 'and we shouldn't find the king's body then.'

'You think it's certain he's there?'

'Very probable. Besides the fact of those three being there, the drawbridge is kept up, and no one goes in without an order from young Hentzau or Black Michael himself. We must tie Fritz up.'

'I'll go to Zenda,' said I.

'You're mad.'

'Some day.'

'Oh, perhaps. You'll very likely stay there though, if you do.'

'That may be, my friend,' said I carelessly.

'His Majesty looks sulky,' observed Sapt. 'How's the love affair?'

'Damn you, hold your tongue!' I said.

He looked at me for a moment, then he lit his pipe. It was quite true that I was in a bad temper, and I went on perversely:

'Wherever I go, I'm dodged by half-a-dozen fellows.'

'I know you are; I send 'em,' he replied composedly.

'What for?'

'Well,' said Sapt, puffing away, 'it wouldn't be exactly inconvenient for Black Michael if you disappeared. With you gone, the old game that we stopped would be played—or he'd have a shot at it.'

'I can take care of myself.'

'De Gautet, Bersonin, and Detchard are in Strelsau; and any one of them, lad, would cut your throat as readily—as readily as I would Black Michael's, and a deal more treacherously. What's the letter?'

I opened it and read it aloud:

'*If the king desires to know what it deeply concerns the king to know, let him do as this letter bids him. At the end of the New Avenue there stands a house in large grounds. The house has a portico, with a statue of a nymph on it. A wall encloses the garden; there is a gate in the wall at the back. At twelve o'clock tonight, if the king enters* alone *by that gate, turns to the right, and walks twenty yards, he will find a summer-house, approached by a flight of six steps. If he mounts and enters, he will find someone who will tell him what touches most dearly his life and his throne. This is written by a faithful friend. He must be alone. If he neglects the invitation his life will be in danger. Let him show this to no one, or he will ruin a woman who loves him: Black Michael does not pardon.*'

'No,' observed Sapt, as I ended, 'but he can dictate a very pretty letter.'

I had arrived at the same conclusion, and was about to throw the letter away, when I saw there was more writing on the other side.

'Hallo! there's some more.'

'*If you hesitate*,' the writer continued, '*consult Colonel Sapt*——'

'Eh!' exclaimed that gentleman, genuinely astonished. 'Does she take me for a greater fool than you?'

I waved him to be silent.

'*Ask him what woman would do most to prevent the duke from marrying his cousin, and therefore most to prevent him becoming king? And ask if her name begins with—A?*'

I sprang to my feet. Sapt laid down his pipe.

'Antoinette de Mauban, by heaven!' I cried.

'How do you know?' asked Sapt.

I told him what I knew of the lady, and how I knew it. He nodded.

'It's so far true that she's had a great row with Michael,' said he, thoughtfully.

'If she would, she could be useful,' I said.

'I believe, though, that Michael wrote that letter.'

'So do I, but I mean to know for certain. I shall go, Sapt.'

'No, I shall go,' said he.

'You may go as far as the gate.'

'I shall go to the summer-house.'

'I'm hanged if you shall!'

I rose and leant my back against the mantelpiece.

'Sapt, I believe in that woman, and I shall go.'

'I don't believe in any woman,' said Sapt, 'and you shan't go.'

'I either go to the summer-house or back to England,' said I.

Sapt began to know exactly how far he could lead or drive, and when he must follow.

'We're playing against time,' I added. 'Every day we leave the king where he is there is fresh risk. Every day I masquerade like this, there is fresh risk. Sapt, we must play high; we must force the game.'

'So be it,' he said, with a sigh.

To cut the story short, at half-past eleven that night Sapt and I mounted our horses. Fritz was again left on guard, our destination not being revealed to him. It was a very dark night. I wore no sword, but I carried a revolver, a long knife, and a bull's-eye lantern.* We arrived outside the gate. I dismounted. Sapt held out his hand.

'I shall wait here,' he said. 'If I hear a shot, I'll——'

'Stay where you are; it's the king's only chance. You mustn't come to grief too.'

'You're right, lad. Good luck!'

I pressed the little gate. It yielded, and I found myself in a wild sort of shrubbery. There was a grass-grown path and, turning to the right as I had been bidden, I followed it cautiously. My lantern was closed, the revolver was in my hand. I heard not a sound. Presently a large dark object loomed out of the gloom ahead of me. It was the summer-house. Reaching the steps, I mounted them and found myself confronted by a weak, rickety wooden door, which hung upon the latch. I pushed it open and walked in. A woman flew to me and seized my hand.

'Shut the door,' she whispered.

I obeyed, and turned the light of my lantern on her. She was in evening dress, arrayed very sumptuously, and her dark striking beauty was marvellously displayed in the glare of the bull's-eye. The summer-house was a bare little room, furnished only with a couple of chairs and a small iron table, such as one sees in a tea-garden or an open-air café.

'Don't talk,' she said. 'We've no time. Listen! I know you, Mr. Rassendyll. I wrote that letter at the duke's orders.'

'So I thought,' said I.

'In twenty minutes three men will be here to kill you.'

'Three—the three?'

'Yes. You must be gone by then. If not, tonight you'll be killed——'

'Or they will.'

'Listen, listen! When you're killed, your body will be taken to a low quarter of the town. It will be found there. Michael will at once arrest all your friends—Colonel Sapt and Captain von Tarlenheim first,—proclaim a state of siege in Strelsau, and send a messenger to Zenda. The other three will murder the king in the Castle, and the duke will proclaim either himself or the princess—himself, if he is strong enough. Anyhow, he'll marry her, and become king in fact, and soon in name. Do you see?'

'It's a pretty plot. But why, madame, do you——?'

'Say I'm a Christian—or say I'm jealous. My God! shall I see him marry her? Now go; but remember—this is what I have to tell you—that never, by night or by day, are you safe. Three men follow you as a guard. Is it not so? Well, three follow them; Michael's three are never two hundred yards from you. Your life is not worth a moment if ever they find you alone. Now go. Stay, the gate will be guarded by now. Go down softly, go past the summer-house, on for a hundred yards, and you'll find a ladder against the wall. Get over it, and fly for your life.'

'And you?' I asked.

'I have my game to play too. If he finds out what I have done, we shall not meet again. If not, I may yet—— But never mind. Go at once.'

'But what will you tell him?'

'That you never came—that you saw through the trick.'

I took her hand and kissed it.

'Madame,' said I, 'you have served the king well tonight. Where is he in the Castle?'

She sank her voice to a fearful whisper. I listened eagerly.

'Across the drawbridge you come to a heavy door; behind that lies——Hark! What's that?'

There were steps outside.

'They're coming! They're too soon. Heavens! they're too soon!' and she turned pale as death.

'They seem to me,' said I, 'to be in the nick of time.'

'Close your lantern. See, there's a chink in the door. Can you see them?'

I put my eye to the chink. On the lowest step I saw three dim figures. I cocked my revolver. Antoinette hastily laid her hand on mine.

'You may kill one,' said she. 'But what then?'

A voice came from outside—a voice that spoke perfect English.

'Mr. Rassendyll,' it said.

I made no answer.

'We want to talk to you. Will you promise not to shoot till we've done?'

'Have I the pleasure of addressing Mr. Detchard?' I said.

'Never mind names.'

'Then let mine alone.'

'All right, *sire*. I've an offer for you.'

I still had my eye to the chink. The three had mounted two steps more; three revolvers pointed full at the door.

'Will you let us in? We pledge our honour to observe the truce.'

'Don't trust them,' whispered Antoinette.

'We can speak through the door,' said I.

'But you might open it and fire,' objected Detchard; 'and though we should finish you, you might finish one of us. Will you give your honour not to fire while we talk?'

'Don't trust them,' whispered Antoinette again.

A sudden idea struck me. I considered it for a moment. It seemed feasible.

'I give my honour not to fire before you do,' said I; 'but I won't let you in. Stand outside and talk.'

'That's sensible,' he said.

The three mounted the last step, and stood just outside the door. I laid my ear to the chink. I could hear no words, but Detchard's head was close to that of the taller of his companions (De Gautet, I guessed).

'H'm! Private communications,' thought I. Then I said aloud:

'Well, gentlemen, what's the offer?'

'A safe-conduct to the frontier, and fifty thousand pounds English.'

'No, no,' whispered Antoinette in the lowest of whispers. 'They are treacherous.'

'That seems handsome,' said I, reconnoitring through the chink. They were all close together, just outside the door now.

I had probed the hearts of the ruffians, and I did not need Antoinette's warning. They meant to 'rush' me as soon as I was engaged in talk.

'Give me a minute to consider,' said I; and I thought I heard a laugh outside.

I turned to Antoinette.

'Stand up close to the wall, out of the line of fire from the door,' I whispered.

'What are you going to do?' she asked in fright.

'You'll see,' said I.

I took up the little iron table. It was not very heavy for a man of my strength, and I held it by the legs. The top, protruding in front of me, made a complete screen for my head and body. I fastened my closed lantern to my belt and put my revolver in a handy pocket. Suddenly I saw the door move ever so slightly—perhaps it was the wind, perhaps it was a hand trying it outside.

I drew back as far as I could from the door, holding the table in the position that I have described. Then I called out:

'Gentlemen, I accept your offer, relying on your honour. If you will open the door——'

'Open it yourself,' said Detchard.

'It opens outwards,' said I. 'Stand back a little, gentlemen, or I shall hit you when I open it.'

I went and fumbled with the latch. Then I stole back to my place on tiptoe.

'I can't open it!' I cried. 'The latch has caught.'

'Tut! I'll open it!' cried Detchard. 'Nonsense, Bersonin, why not? Are you afraid of one man?'

I smiled to myself. An instant later the door was flung back. The gleam of a lantern showed me the three close together outside, their revolvers levelled. With a shout, I charged at my utmost pace across the summer-house and through the doorway. Three shots rang out and battered into my shield. Another moment, and I leapt out and the table caught them full and square, and in a tumbling, swearing, struggling mass they and I and that brave table rolled down the steps of the summer-house to the ground below. Antoinette de Mauban shrieked, but I rose to my feet, laughing aloud.

De Gautet and Bersonin lay like men stunned. Detchard was under the table, but, as I rose, he pushed it from him and fired again. I raised my revolver and took a snap shot*; I heard him curse, and then I ran like a hare, laughing as I went, past the summer-house and along by the wall. I heard steps behind me, and turning round I fired again for luck. The steps ceased.

'Please God,' said I, 'she told me the truth about the ladder!' for the wall was high and topped with iron spikes.

Yes, there it was. I was up and over in a minute. Doubling back, I saw the horses; then I heard a shot. It was Sapt. He had heard us, and was battling and raging with the locked gate, hammering it and firing into the keyhole, like a man possessed. He had quite forgotten that he was not to take part in the fight. Whereat I laughed again, and said, as I clapped him on the shoulder:

'Come home to bed, old chap. I've got the finest tea-table story that ever you heard!'

He started and cried: 'You're safe!' and wrung my hand. But a moment later he added:

'And what the devil are you laughing at?'

'Four gentlemen round a tea-table,' said I, laughing still, for it had been uncommonly ludicrous to see the formidable three altogether routed and scattered with no more deadly weapon than an ordinary tea-table.

Moreover, you will observe that I had honourably kept my word, and not fired till they did.

CHAPTER X

A GREAT CHANCE FOR A VILLAIN

It was the custom that the Prefect of Police should send every after-noon a report to me on the condition of the capital and the feeling of the people: the document included also an account of the movements of any persons whom the police had received instructions to watch. Since I had been in Strelsau, Sapt had been in the habit of reading the report and telling me any items of interest which it might contain. On the day after my adventure in the summer-house, he came in as I was playing a hand of *écarté** with Fritz von Tarlenheim.

'The report is rather full of interest this afternoon,' he observed, sitting down.

'Do you find,' I asked, 'any mention of a certain *fracas*?'

He shook his head with a smile.

'I find this first,' he said: '"His Highness the Duke of Strelsau left the city (so far as it appears, suddenly), accompanied by several of his household. His destination is believed to be the Castle of Zenda, but the party travelled by road and not by train. MM. De Gautet, Bersonin and Detchard followed an hour later, the last-named carry-ing his arm in a sling. The cause of his wound is not known, but it is suspected that he has fought a duel, probably incidental to a love affair."'

'That is remotely true,' I observed, very well pleased to find that I had left my mark on the fellow.

'Then we come to this,' pursued Sapt: '"Madame de Mauban, whose movements have been watched according to instructions, left by train at midday. She took a ticket for Dresden——"'

'It's an old habit of hers,' said I.

'"The Dresden trains stop at Zenda." An acute fellow, this. And finally listen to this: "The state of feeling in the city is not satisfactory. The king is much criticised" (you know, he's told to be quite frank) "for taking no steps about his marriage. From enquiries among the *entourage* of the Princess Flavia, her Royal Highness is believed to be deeply offended by the remissness of his Majesty. The common people are coupling her name with that of the Duke of Strelsau, and the duke gains much popularity from the suggestion. I have caused the announcement that the king gives a ball tonight in honour of the princess to be widely diffused, and the effect is good."'

'That is news to me,' said I.

'Oh, the preparations are all made!' laughed Fritz. 'I've seen to that.'

Sapt turned to me and said, in a sharp, decisive voice:

'You must make love to her* tonight, you know.'

'I think it very likely I shall, if I see her alone,' said I. 'Hang it, Sapt, you don't suppose I find it difficult?'

Fritz whistled a bar or two; then he said:

'You'll find it only too easy. Look here, I hate telling you this, but I must. The Countess Helga told me that the princess had become most attached to the king. Since the coronation, her feelings have undergone a marked development. It's quite true that she is deeply wounded by the king's apparent neglect.'

'Here's a kettle of fish!' I groaned.

'Tut, tut!' said Sapt. 'I suppose you've made pretty speeches to a girl before now? That's all she wants.'

Fritz, himself a lover, understood better my distress. He laid his hand on my shoulder, but said nothing.

'I think, though,' pursued that cold-blooded old Sapt, 'that you'd better make your offer tonight.'

'Good heavens!'

'Or, at any rate, go near it: and I shall send a "semi-official" to the papers.'

'I'll do nothing of the sort—no more will you!' said I. 'I utterly refuse to take part in making a fool of the princess.'

Sapt looked at me with his small keen eyes. A slow cunning smile passed over his face.

'All right, lad, all right,' said he. 'We mustn't press you too hard. Soothe her down a bit, if you can, you know. Now for Michael!'

'Oh, damn Michael!' said I. 'He'll do tomorrow. Here, Fritz, come for a stroll in the garden.'

Sapt at once yielded. His rough manner covered a wonderful tact—and, as I came to recognise more and more, a remarkable knowledge of human nature. Why did he urge me so little about the princess? Because he knew that her beauty and my ardour would carry me further than all his arguments—and the less I thought about the thing, the more likely was I to do it. He must have seen the unhappiness he might bring on the princess; but that went for nothing with him. Can I say, confidently, that he was wrong? If the king were restored, the princess must turn to him, either knowing or not knowing the change. And if the king were not restored to us? It was a subject that we had never yet spoken of. But I had an idea that, in such a case, Sapt meant to seat me on the throne of Ruritania for the term of my life. He would have set Satan himself there sooner than that pupil of his, Black Michael.

The ball was a sumptuous affair. I opened it by dancing a quadrille* with Flavia: then I waltzed with her. Curious eyes and eager whispers attended us. We went in to supper; and, half-way through, I, half-mad by then, for her glance had answered mine, and her quick breathing met my stammered sentences,—I rose in my place before all the brilliant crowd, and taking the Red Rose that I wore, flung the ribbon with its jewelled badge round her neck. In a tumult of applause I sat down: I saw Sapt smiling over his wine, and Fritz frowning. The rest of the meal passed in silence; neither Flavia nor I could speak. Fritz touched me on the shoulder, and I rose, gave her my arm, and walked down the hall into a little room, where coffee was served to us. The gentlemen and ladies in attendance withdrew, and we were alone.

The little room had French windows opening on the gardens. The night was fine, cool, and fragrant. Flavia sat down, and I stood opposite her. I was struggling with myself: if she had not looked at me, I believe that even then I should have won my fight. But suddenly, involuntarily, she gave me one brief glance—a glance of question, hurriedly turned aside; a blush that the question had ever come spread over her cheek, and she caught her breath. Ah, if you had seen her! I forgot the king in Zenda. I forgot the king in Strelsau. She was a princess—and I an impostor. Do you think I remembered that? I threw myself on my knee and seized her hands in mine. I said nothing. Why should I? The soft sounds of the night set my wooing to a wordless melody, as I pressed my kisses on her lips.

She pushed me from her, crying suddenly:

'Ah! is it true? or is it only because you must?'

'It's true!' I said, in low smothered tones,—'true that I love you more than life—or truth—or honour!'

She set no meaning to my words, treating them as one of love's sweet extravagances. She came close to me, and whispered:

'Oh, if you were not the king! Then I could show you how I love you! How is it that I love you now, Rudolf?'

'Now?'

'Yes—just lately. I—I never did before.'

Pure triumph filled me. It was I—Rudolf Rassendyll—who had won her! I caught her round the waist.

'You didn't love me before?' I asked.

She looked up into my face, smiling, as she whispered:

'It must have been your Crown. I felt it first on the Coronation Day.'

'Never before?' I asked eagerly.

She laughed low.

'You speak as if you would be pleased to hear me say "Yes" to that,' she said.

'Would "Yes" be true?'

'Yes,' I just heard her breathe, and she went on in an instant: 'Be careful, Rudolf; be careful, dear. He will be mad now.'

'What, Michael? If Michael were the worst——'

'What worse is there?'

There was yet a chance for me. Controlling myself with a mighty effort, I took my hands off her and stood a yard or two away. I remember now the note of the wind in the elm-trees outside.

'If I were not the king,' I began, 'if I were only a private gentleman——'

Before I could finish, her hand was in mine.

'If you were a convict in the prison of Strelsau, you would be my king,' she said.

And under my breath I groaned 'God forgive me!' and, holding her hand in mine, I said again:

'If I were not the king——'

'Hush, hush!' she whispered. 'I don't deserve it—I don't deserve to be doubted. Ah, Rudolf! does a woman who marries without love look on the man as I look on you?'

And she hid her face from me.

For more than a minute we stood there together; and I, even with my arm about her, summoned up what honour and conscience her beauty and the toils* that I was in had left me.

'Flavia,' I said, in a strange, dry voice that seemed not my own. 'I am not——'

As I spoke—as she raised her eyes to me—there was a heavy step on the gravel outside, and a man appeared at the window. A little cry burst from Flavia, as she sprang back from me. My half-finished sentence died on my lips. Sapt stood there, bowing low, but with a stern frown on his face.

'A thousand pardons, sire,' said he, 'but his Eminence the Cardinal has waited this quarter of an hour to offer his respectful adieu to your Majesty.'

I met his eye full and square; and I read in it an angry warning. How long he had been a listener I knew not, but he had come in upon us in the nick of time.

'We must not keep his Eminence waiting,' said I.

But Flavia, in whose love there lay no shame, with radiant eyes and blushing face, held out her hand to Sapt. She said nothing, but no man could have missed her meaning who had ever seen a woman in the exultation of love. A sour, yet sad, smile passed on the old soldier's face, and there was tenderness in his voice as, bending to kiss her hand, he said:

'In joy and sorrow, in good times and bad, God save your Royal Highness!'

He paused and added, glancing at me and drawing himself up to military erectness:

'But, before all comes the king—God save the King!'

And Flavia caught at my hand and kissed it, murmuring:

'Amen! Good God, Amen!'

We went into the ball-room again. Forced to receive adieus, I was separated from Flavia: everyone, when they left me, went to her. Sapt was out and in of the throng, and where he had been, glances, smiles, and whispers were rife. I doubted not that, true to his relentless purpose, he was spreading the news that he had learnt. To uphold the Crown and beat Black Michael—that was his one resolve. Flavia, myself—ay, and the real king in Zenda, were pieces in his game; and pawns have no business with passions. Not even at the walls of the Palace did he stop; for when at last I handed Flavia down the broad marble steps and into her carriage, there was a great crowd awaiting us, and we were welcomed with deafening cheers. What could I do? Had I spoken then, they would have refused to believe that I was not the king; they might have believed that the king had run mad. By Sapt's devices and my own ungoverned passion I had been forced on, and the way back had closed behind me; and the passion still drove me in the same direction as the devices seduced me. I faced all Strelsau that night as the king and the accepted suitor of the Princess Flavia.

At last, at three in the morning, when the cold light of dawning day began to steal in, I was in my dressing-room, and Sapt alone was with me. I sat like a man dazed, staring into the fire; he puffed at his pipe; Fritz was gone to bed, having almost refused to speak to me. On the table by me lay a rose; it had been in Flavia's dress, and, as we parted, she had kissed it and given it to me.

Sapt advanced his hand towards the rose, but, with a quick movement, I shut mine down upon it.

'That's mine,' I said, 'not yours—nor the king's either.'

'We struck a good blow for the king tonight,' said he.

I turned on him fiercely.

'What's to prevent me striking a blow for myself?' I said.

He nodded his head.

'I know what's in your mind,' he said. 'Yes, lad; but you're bound in honour.'

'Have you left me any honour?'

'Oh, come, to play a little trick on a girl——'

'You can spare me that. Colonel Sapt, if you would not have me utterly a villain—if you would not have your king rot in Zenda, while Michael and I play for the great stake outside——You follow me?'

'Ay, I follow you.'

'We must act, and quickly! You saw tonight—you heard tonight——'

'I did,' said he.

'Your cursed acuteness told you what I should do. Well, leave me here a week—and there's another problem for you. Do you find the answer?'

'Yes, I find it,' he answered, frowning heavily. 'But if you did that, you'd have to fight me first—and kill me.'

'Well, and if I had—or a score of men? I tell you, I could raise all Strelsau on you in an hour, and choke you with your lies—yes, your mad lies—in your mouth.'

'It's gospel truth,' he said,—'thanks to my advice, you could.'

'I could marry the princess, and send Michael and his brother together to——'

'I'm not denying it, lad,' said he.

'Then, in God's name,' I cried, stretching out my hands to him, 'let us go to Zenda and crush this Michael, and bring the king back to his own again.'

The old fellow stood and looked at me for full a minute.

'And the princess?' he said.

I bowed my head to meet my hands, and crushed the rose between my fingers and my lips.

I felt his hand on my shoulder, and his voice sounded husky as he whispered low in my ear:

'Before God, you're the finest Elphberg of them all. But I have eaten of the king's bread, and I am the king's servant. Come, we will go to Zenda!'

And I looked up and caught him by the hand. And the eyes of both of us were wet.

CHAPTER XI

HUNTING A VERY BIG BOAR

THE terrible temptation which was assailing me will now be understood. I could so force Michael's hand that he must kill the king. I was in a position to bid him defiance and tighten my grasp on the crown—not for its own sake, but because the King of Ruritania was to wed the Princess Flavia. What of Sapt and Fritz? Ah! but a man cannot be held to write down in cold blood the wild and black thoughts that storm his brain when an uncontrolled passion has battered a breach for them. Yet, unless he sets up as a saint, he need not hate himself for them. He is better employed, as it humbly seems to me, in giving thanks that power to resist was vouchsafed to him, than in fretting over wicked impulses which come unsought and extort an unwilling hospitality from the weakness of our nature.

It was a fine bright morning when I walked, unattended, to the princess's house, carrying a nosegay* in my hand. Policy made excuses for love, and every attention that I paid her, while it riveted my own chains, bound closer to me the people of the great city, who worshipped her. I found Fritz's *inamorata*,* the Countess Helga, gathering blooms in the garden for her mistress's wear, and prevailed on her to take mine in their place. The girl was rosy with happiness, for Fritz, in his turn, had not wasted his evening, and no dark shadow hung over his wooing, save the hatred which the Duke of Strelsau was known to bear him.

'And that,' she said, with a mischievous smile, 'your Majesty has made of no moment. Yes, I will take the flowers; shall I tell you, sire, what is the first thing the princess does with them?'

We were talking on a broad terrace that ran along the back of the house, and a window above our heads stood open.

'Madame!' cried the countess merrily, and Flavia herself looked out. I bared my head and bowed. She wore a white gown, and her hair was loosely gathered in a knot. She kissed her hand to me, crying:

'Bring the king up, Helga; I'll give him some coffee.'

The countess, with a gay glance, led the way, and took me into Flavia's morning-room. And, left alone, we greeted one another as lovers are wont. Then the princess laid two letters before me. One was from Black Michael—a most courteous request that she would honour him by spending a day at his Castle of Zenda, as had been her custom once a year in the summer, when the place and its gardens were in the height of their great beauty. I threw the letter down in disgust, and Flavia laughed at me. Then, growing grave again, she pointed to the other sheet.

'I don't know who that comes from,' she said. 'Read it.'

I knew in a moment. There was no signature at all this time, but the handwriting was the same as that which had told me of the snare in the summer-house; it was Antoinette de Mauban's.

'*I have no cause to love you*,' it ran, '*but God forbid that you should fall into the power of the duke. Accept no invitations of his. Go nowhere without a large guard—a regiment is not too much to make you safe. Show this, if you can, to him who reigns in Strelsau.*'

'Why doesn't it say "the king"?' asked Flavia, leaning over my shoulder, so that the ripple of her hair played on my cheek. 'Is it a hoax?'

'As you value life, and more than life, my queen,' I said, 'obey it to the very letter. A regiment shall camp round your house today. See that you do not go out unless well guarded.'

'An order, sire?' she asked, a little rebellious.

'Yes, an order, madame—if you love me.'

'Ah!' she cried; and I could not but kiss her.

'You know who sent it?' she asked.

'I guess,' said I. 'It is from a good friend—and, I fear, an unhappy woman. You must be ill, Flavia, and unable to go to Zenda. Make your excuses as cold and formal as you like.'

'So you feel strong enough to anger Michael?' she said, with a proud smile.

'I'm strong enough for anything, while you are safe,' said I.

Soon I tore myself away from her, and then, without consulting Sapt, I took my way to the house of Marshal Strakencz. I had seen something of the old general, and I liked and trusted him. Sapt was less enthusiastic, but I had learnt by now that Sapt was best pleased when he could do everything, and jealousy played some part in his views. As things were now, I had more work than Sapt and Fritz could manage, for they must come with me to Zenda, and I wanted a man to guard what I loved most in all the world, and suffer me to set about my task of releasing the king with a quiet mind.

The Marshal received me with most loyal kindness. To some extent, I took him into my confidence. I charged him with the care of the princess, looking him full and significantly in the face as I bade him let no one from her cousin the duke approach her, unless he himself were there and a dozen of his men with him.

'You may be right, sire,' said he, shaking his grey head sadly. 'I have known better men than the duke do worse things than that for love.'

I could quite appreciate the remark, but I said:

'There's something beside love, Marshal. Love's for the heart; is there nothing my brother might like for his head?'

'I pray that you wrong him, sire.'

'Marshal, I'm leaving Strelsau for a few days. Every evening I will send a courier to you. If for three days none comes, you will publish an order which I will give you, depriving Duke Michael of the governorship of Strelsau and appointing you in his place. You will declare a state of siege. Then you will send word to Michael that you demand an audience of the king——You follow me?'

'Ay, sire.'

'——In twenty-four hours. If he does not produce the king' (I laid my hand on his knee), 'then the king is dead, and you will proclaim the next heir. You know who that is?'

'The Princess Flavia.'

'And swear to me, on your faith and honour and by the fear of the living God, that you will stand by her to your death, and kill that reptile, and seat her where I sit now.'

'On my faith and honour, and by the fear of God, I swear it! And may Almighty God preserve your Majesty, for I think that you go on an errand of danger.'

'I hope that no life more precious than mine may be demanded,' said I, rising. Then I held out my hand to him.

'Marshal,' I said, 'in days to come, it may be—I know not—that you will hear strange things of the man who speaks to you now. Let him be what he may, and who he may, what say you of the manner in which he has borne himself as king in Strelsau?'

The old man, holding my hand, spoke to me, man to man.

'I have known many of the Elphbergs,' said he, 'and I have seen you. And, happen what may, you have borne yourself as a wise king and a brave man; ay, and you have proved as courteous a gentleman and as gallant a lover as any that have been of the House.'

'Be that my epitaph,' said I, 'when the time comes that another sits on the throne of Ruritania.'

'God send a far day, and may I not see it!' said he.

I was much moved, and the Marshal's worn face twitched. I sat down and wrote my order.

'I can hardly yet write,' said I; 'my finger is stiff still.'

It was, in fact, the first time that I had ventured to write more than a signature; and in spite of the pains I had taken to learn the king's hand, I was not yet perfect in it.

'Indeed, sire,' he said, 'it differs a little from your ordinary hand-writing. It is unfortunate, for it may lead to a suspicion of forgery.'

'Marshal,' said I, with a laugh, 'what use are the guns of Strelsau, if they can't assuage a little suspicion?'

He smiled grimly, and took the paper.

'Colonel Sapt and Fritz von Tarlenheim go with me,' I continued.

'You go to seek the duke?' he asked in a low tone.

'Yes, the duke, and someone else of whom I have need, and who is at Zenda,' I replied.

'I wish I could go with you,' he cried, tugging at his white moustache. 'I'd like to strike a blow for you and your crown.'

'I leave you what is more than my life and more than my crown,' said I, 'because you are the man I trust more than all others in Ruritania.'

'I will deliver her to you safe and sound,' said he, 'and, failing that, I will make her queen.'

We parted, and I returned to the Palace and told Sapt and Fritz what I had done. Sapt had a few faults to find and a few grumbles to utter. This was merely what I expected, for Sapt liked to be consulted beforehand, not informed afterwards; but on the whole he approved of my plans, and his spirits rose high as the hour of action drew nearer and nearer. Fritz, too, was ready; though he, poor fellow, risked more than Sapt did, for he was a lover, and his happiness hung in the scale. Yet how I envied him! For the triumphant issue which would crown him with happiness and unite him to his mistress, the success for which we were bound to hope and strive and struggle, meant to me sorrow more certain and greater than if I were doomed to fail. He understood something of this, for when we were alone (save for old Sapt, who was smoking at the other end of the room) he passed his arm through mine, saying:

'It's hard for you. Don't think I don't trust you; I know you have nothing but true thoughts in your heart.'

But I turned away from him, thankful that he could not see what my heart held, but only be witness to the deeds that my hands were to do.

Yet even he did not understand, for he had not dared to lift his eyes to the Princess Flavia, as I had lifted mine.

Our plans were now all made, even as we proceeded to carry them out, and as they will hereafter appear. The next morning we were to start on the hunting excursion. I had made all arrangements for being absent, and now there was only one thing left to do—the hardest, the most heart-breaking. As evening fell, I drove through the busy streets to Flavia's residence. I was recognised as I went and heartily cheered. I played my part, and made shift to look the happy lover. In spite of my depression, I was almost amused at the coolness and delicate *hauteur* with which my sweet lover received me. She had heard that the king was leaving Strelsau on a hunting expedition.

'I regret that we cannot amuse your Majesty here in Strelsau,' she said, tapping her foot lightly on the floor. 'I would have offered you more entertainment, but I was foolish enough to think——'

'Well, what?' I asked, leaning over her.

'That for just a day or two, after—after last night—you might be happy without much gaiety;' and she turned pettishly from me, as she added, 'I hope the boars will be more engrossing.'

'I'm going after a very big boar,' said I; and, because I could not help it, I began to play with her hair, but she moved her head away.

'Are you offended with me?' I asked, in feigned surprise, for I could not resist tormenting her a little. I had never seen her angry, and every fresh aspect of her was a delight to me.

'What right have I to be offended? True, you said last night that every hour away from me was wasted. But a very big boar! that's a different thing.'

'Perhaps the boar will hunt me,' I suggested. 'Perhaps, Flavia, he'll catch me.'

She made no answer.

'You are not touched even by that danger?'

Still she said nothing; and I, stealing round, found her eyes full of tears.

'You weep for my danger?'

Then she spoke very low:

'This is like what you used to be; but not like the king—the king I—I have come to love!'

With a sudden great groan, I caught her to my heart.

'My darling!' I cried, forgetting everything but her, 'did you dream that I left you to go hunting?'

'What then, Rudolf? Ah! you're not going——?'

'Well, it is hunting. I go to seek Michael in his lair.'

She had turned very pale.

'So you see, sweet, I was not so poor a lover as you thought me. I shall not be long gone.'

'You will write to me, Rudolf?'

I was weak, but I could not say a word to stir suspicion in her.

'I'll send you all my heart every day,' said I.

'And you'll run no danger?'

'None that I need not.'

'And when will you be back? Ah, how long it will be!'

'When shall I be back?' I repeated.

'Yes, yes! Don't be long, dear, don't be long. I shan't sleep while you're away.'

'I don't know when I shall be back,' said I.

'Soon, Rudolf, soon.'

'God knows, my darling. But, if never——'

'Hush, hush!' and she pressed her lips to mine.

'If never,' I whispered, 'you must take my place; you'll be the only one of the House then. You must reign, and not weep for me.'

For a moment she drew herself up like a very queen.

'Yes, I will!' she said. 'I will reign. I will do my part, though all my life will be empty and my heart dead; yet I'll do it.'

She paused, and sinking against me again, wailed softly:

'Come soon! come soon!'

Carried away, I cried loudly:

'As God lives, I—yes, I myself—will see you once more before I die.'

'What do you mean?' she exclaimed, with wondering eyes; but I had no answer for her, and she gazed at me with her wondering eyes.

I dared not ask her to forget, she would have found it an insult. I could not tell her then who and what I was. She was weeping, and I had but to dry her tears.

'Shall a man not come back to the loveliest lady in all the wide world?' said I. 'A thousand Michaels should not keep me from you!'

She clung to me, a little comforted.

'You won't let Michael hurt you?'

'No, sweetheart.'

'Or keep you from me?'

'No, sweetheart.'

'Nor anyone else?'

And again I answered:

'No, sweetheart.'

Yet there was one—not Michael—who, if he lived, must keep me from her; and for whose life I was going forth to stake my own. And his figure—the lithe, buoyant figure I had met in the woods of Zenda—the dull, inert mass I had left in the cellar of the shooting-lodge—seemed to rise, double-shaped, before me, and to come between us, thrusting itself in even where she lay, pale, exhausted, fainting, in my arms, and yet looking up at me with those eyes that bore such love as I have never seen, and haunt me now, and will till the ground closes over me—and (who knows?) perhaps beyond.

CHAPTER XII

I RECEIVE A VISITOR AND BAIT A HOOK

ABOUT five miles from Zenda—on the opposite side from that on which the Castle is situated, there lies a large tract of wood. It is rising ground, and in the centre of the demesne,* on the top of the hill, stands a fine modern *château*, the property of a distant kinsman of Fritz's, the Count Stanislas von Tarlenheim. Count Stanislas himself was a student and a recluse. He seldom visited the house, and had, on Fritz's request, very readily and courteously offered me its hospitality for myself and my party. This, then, was our destination; chosen ostensibly for the sake of the boar-hunting (for the wood was carefully preserved, and boars, once common all over Ruritania, were still to be found there in considerable numbers*), really because it brought us within striking distance of the Duke of Strelsau's more magnificent dwelling on the other side of the town. A large party of servants, with horses and luggage, started early in the morning; we followed at midday, travelling by train for thirty miles, and then mounting our horses to ride the remaining distance to the *château*.

We were a gallant party. Besides Sapt and Fritz, I was accompanied by ten gentlemen: every one of them had been carefully chosen, and no less carefully sounded, by my two friends, and all were devotedly attached to the person of the king. They were told a part of the truth: the attempt on my life in the summer-house was revealed to them, as a spur to their loyalty and an incitement against Michael. They were also informed that a friend of the king's was suspected to be forcibly confined within the Castle of Zenda. His rescue was one of the objects of the expedition; but, it was added, the king's main desire was to carry into effect certain steps against his treacherous brother, as to the precise nature of which they could not at present be further enlightened. Enough that the king commanded their services, and would rely on their devotion when occasion arose to call for it. Young, well-bred, brave, and loyal, they asked no more: they were ready to prove their dutiful obedience, and prayed for a fight as the best and most exhilarating mode of showing it.

Thus the scene was shifted from Strelsau to the *château* of Tarlenheim and Castle of Zenda, which frowned at us across the valley. I tried to shift my thoughts also, to forget my love, and to bend all my energies to the task before me. It was to get the king out of the Castle alive. Force was useless: in some trick lay the chance; and I had already an inkling of what we must do. But I was terribly hampered by the publicity which attended my movements. Michael must know by now of my expedition; and I knew Michael too well to suppose that his eyes would be blinded by the feint of the boar-hunt. He would understand very well what the real quarry was. That, however, must be risked—that and all it might mean; for Sapt, no less than myself, recognised that the present state of things had become unendurable. And there was one thing that I dared to calculate on—not, as I now know, without warrant. It was this—that Black Michael would not believe that I meant well by the king. He could not appreciate—I will not say an honest man, for the thoughts of my own heart have been revealed—but a man acting honestly. He saw my opportunity as I had seen it, as Sapt had seen it; he knew the princess—nay (and I declare that a sneaking sort of pity for him invaded me), in his way he loved her; he would think that Sapt and Fritz could be bribed, so the bribe were large enough. Thinking thus, would he kill the king, my rival and my danger? Ay, verily, that he would, with as little compunction as he would kill a rat. But he would kill Rudolf Rassendyll first, if he could; and nothing but the certainty of being utterly damned by the release of the king alive and his restoration to the throne would drive him to throw away the trump card which he held in reserve to baulk the supposed game of the impudent impostor Rassendyll. Musing on all this as I rode along, I took courage.

Michael knew of my coming, sure enough. I had not been in the house an hour, when an imposing Embassy arrived from him. He did not quite reach the impudence of sending my would-be assassins, but he sent the other three of his famous Six—the three Ruritanian gentlemen—Lauengram, Krafstein, and Rupert Hentzau. A fine, strapping trio they were, splendidly horsed and admirably equipped. Young Rupert, who looked a dare-devil, and could not have been more than twenty-two or twenty-three, took the lead, and made us the neatest speech, wherein my devoted subject and loving brother,

Michael of Strelsau, prayed me to pardon him for not paying his addresses in person, and, further, for not putting his Castle at my disposal; the reason for both of these apparent derelictions being that he and several of his servants lay sick of scarlet fever, and were in a very sad, and also a very infectious, state. So declared young Rupert with an insolent smile on his curling upper-lip and a toss of his thick hair—he was a handsome villain, and the gossip ran that many a lady had troubled her heart for him already.

'If my brother has scarlet fever,' said I, 'he is nearer my complexion than he is wont to be, my lord. I trust he does not suffer?'

'He is able to attend to his affairs, sire.'

'I hope all beneath your roof are not sick. What of my good friends, De Gautet, Bersonin, and Detchard? I heard the last had suffered a hurt.'

Lauengram and Krafstein looked glum and uneasy, but young Rupert's smile grew broader.

'He hopes soon to find a medicine for it, sire,' he answered.

And I burst out laughing, for I knew what medicine Detchard longed for—it is called Revenge.

'You will dine with us, gentlemen?' I asked.

Young Rupert was profuse in apologies. They had urgent duties at the Castle.

'Then,' said I, with a wave of my hand, 'to our next meeting, gentlemen. May it make us better acquainted.'

'We will pray your Majesty for an early opportunity,' quoth Rupert airily; and he strode past Sapt with such jeering scorn on his face that I saw the old fellow clench his fist and scowl black as night.

For my part, if a man must needs be a knave, I would have him a debonair knave, and I liked Rupert Hentzau better than his long-faced close-eyed companions. It makes your sin no worse, as I conceive, to do it *à la mode* and stylishly.

Now it was a curious thing that on this first night, instead of eating the excellent dinner my cooks had prepared for me, I must needs leave my gentlemen to eat it alone, under Sapt's presiding care, and ride myself with Fritz to the town of Zenda and a certain little inn that I knew of. There was little danger in the excursion; the evenings were long and light, and the road this side of Zenda well frequented. So off we rode, with a groom behind us. I muffled myself up in a big cloak.

'Fritz,' said I, as we entered the town, 'there's an uncommonly pretty girl at this inn.'

'How do you know?' he asked.

'Because I've been there,' said I.

'Since——?' he began.

'No. Before,' said I.

'But they'll recognise you?'

'Well, of course they will. Now, don't argue, my good fellow, but listen to me. We're two gentlemen of the king's household, and one of us has a toothache. The other will order a private room and dinner, and, further, a bottle of the best wine for the sufferer. And if he be as clever a fellow as I take him for, the pretty girl and no other will wait on us.'

'What if she won't?' objected Fritz.

'My dear Fritz,' said I, 'if she won't for you, she will for me.'

We were at the inn. Nothing of me but my eyes was visible as I walked in. The landlady received us; two minutes later, my little friend (ever, I fear me, on the look out for such guests as might prove amusing) made her appearance. Dinner and the wine were ordered. I sat down in the private room. A minute later Fritz came in.

'She's coming,' he said.

'If she were not, I should have to doubt the Countess Helga's taste.'

She came in. I gave her time to set the wine down—I didn't want it dropped. Fritz poured out a glass and gave it to me.

'Is the gentleman in great pain?' the girl asked, sympathetically.

'The gentleman is no worse than when he saw you last,' said I, throwing away my cloak.

She started, with a little shriek. Then she cried:

'It was the king, then! I told mother so the moment I saw his picture. Oh, sir, forgive me!'

'Faith, you gave me nothing that hurt much,' said I.

'But the things we said!'

'I forgive them for the thing you did.'

'I must go and tell mother.'

'Stop,' said I, assuming a graver air. 'We are not here for sport tonight. Go and bring dinner, and not a word of the king being here.'

She came back in a few minutes, looking grave, yet very curious.

'Well, how is Johann?' I asked, beginning my dinner.

'Oh, that fellow, sir—my lord king, I mean!'

'"Sir" will do, please. How is he?'

'We hardly see him now, sir.'

'And why not?'

'I told him he came too often, sir,' said she, tossing her head.

'So he sulks and stays away?'

'Yes, sir.'

'But you could bring him back?' I suggested, with a smile.

'Perhaps I could,' said she.

'I know your powers, you see,' said I, and she blushed with pleasure.

'It's not only that, sir, that keeps him away. He's very busy at the Castle.'

'But there's no shooting on now.'

'No, sir; but he's in charge of the house.'

'Johann turned housemaid?'

The little girl was brimming over with gossip.

'Well, there are no others,' said she. 'There's not a woman there—not as a servant, I mean. They do say—but perhaps it's false, sir.'

'Let's have it for what it's worth,' said I.

'Indeed, I'm ashamed to tell you, sir.'

'Oh, see, I'm looking at the ceiling.'

'They do say there is a lady there, sir; but, except for her, there's not a woman in the place. And Johann has to wait on the gentlemen.'

'Poor Johann! He must be overworked. Yet I'm sure he could find half-an-hour to come and see you.'

'It would depend on the time, sir, perhaps.'

'Do you love him?' I asked.

'Not I, sir.'

'And you wish to serve the king?'

'Yes, sir.'

'Then tell him to meet you at the second milestone out of Zenda tomorrow evening at ten o'clock. Say you'll be there and will walk home with him.'

'Do you mean him harm, sir?'

'Not if he will do as I bid him. But I think I've told you enough, my pretty maid. See that you do as I bid you. And, mind, no one is to know that the king has been here.'

I spoke a little sternly, for there is seldom harm in infusing a little fear into a woman's liking for you, and I softened the effect by giving her a handsome present. Then we dined, and, wrapping my cloak about my face, with Fritz leading the way, we went downstairs to our horses again.

It was but half-past eight, and hardly yet dark; the streets were full for such a quiet little place, and I could see that gossip was all agog. With the king on one side and the duke on the other, Zenda felt itself the centre of all Ruritania. We jogged gently through the town, but set our horses to a sharper pace when we reached the open country.

'You want to catch this fellow Johann?' asked Fritz.

'Ay, and I fancy I've baited the hook right. Our little Delilah will bring our Samson.* It is not enough, Fritz, to have no women in a house, though brother Michael shows some wisdom there. If you want safety, you must have none within fifty miles.'

'None nearer than Strelsau, for instance,' said poor Fritz, with a lovelorn sigh.

We reached the avenue of the *château*, and were soon at the house. As the hoofs of our horses sounded on the gravel, Sapt rushed out to meet us.

'Thank God, you're safe!' he cried. 'Have you seen anything of them?'

'Of whom?' I asked, dismounting.

He drew us aside, that the grooms might not hear.

'Lad,' he said to me, 'you must not ride about here, unless with half-a-dozen of us. You know among our men a tall young fellow, Bernenstein by name?'

I knew him. He was a fine strapping young man, almost of my height, and of light complexion.

'He lies in his room upstairs, with a bullet through his arm.'

'The deuce he does!'

'After dinner he strolled out alone, and went a mile or so into the wood; and as he walked, he thought he saw three men among the trees; and one levelled a gun at him. He had no weapon, and he started at a run back towards the house. But one of them fired, and he was hit, and had much ado to reach here before he fainted. By good luck, they feared to pursue him nearer the house.'

He paused, and added:

'Lad, the bullet was meant for you.'

'It is very likely,' said I, 'and it's first blood to brother Michael.'

'I wonder which three it was,' said Fritz.

'Well, Sapt,' I said, 'I went out tonight for no idle purpose, as you shall hear. But there's one thing in my mind.'

'What's that?' he asked.

'Why this,' I answered. 'That I shall ill requite the very great honours Ruritania has done me if I depart from it, leaving one of those Six alive—neither, with the help of God, will I.'

And Sapt shook my hand on that.

CHAPTER XIII

AN IMPROVEMENT ON JACOB'S LADDER

IN the morning of the day after that on which I swore my oath against the Six, I gave certain orders, and then rested in greater contentment than I had known for some time. I was at work; and work, though it cannot cure love, is yet a narcotic to it; so that Sapt, who grew feverish, marvelled to see me sprawling in an arm-chair in the sunshine, listening to one of my friends who sang me amorous songs in a mellow voice and induced in me a pleasing melancholy. Thus was I engaged when young Rupert Hentzau, who feared neither man nor devil, and rode through the demesne—where every tree might hide a marksman, for all he knew—as though it had been the park at Strelsau, cantered up to where I lay, bowing with burlesque deference, and craving private speech with me in order to deliver a message from the Duke of Strelsau. I made all withdraw, and then he said, seating himself by me:

'The king is in love, it seems?'

'Not with life, my lord,' said I, smiling.

'It is well,' he rejoined. 'Come, we are alone. Rassendyll——'

I rose to a sitting posture.

'What's the matter?' he asked.

'I was about to call one of my gentlemen to bring your horse, my lord. If you do not know how to address the king, my brother must find another messenger.'

'Why keep up the farce?' he asked, negligently dusting his boot with his glove.

'Because it is not finished yet; and meanwhile I'll choose my own name.'

'Oh, so be it! Yet I spoke in love for you; for indeed you are a man after my own heart.'

'Saving my poor honesty,' said I, 'maybe I am. But that I keep faith with men, and honour with women, maybe I am, my lord.'

He darted a glance at me—a glance of anger.

'Is your mother dead?' said I.

'Ay, she's dead.'

'She may thank God,' said I, and I heard him curse me softly. 'Well, what's the message?' I continued.

I had touched him on the raw, for all the world knew he had broken his mother's heart and flaunted his mistresses in her house; and his airy manner was gone for the moment.

'The duke offers you more than I would,' he growled. 'A halter for you, *sire*, was my suggestion. But he offers you safe-conduct across the frontier and a million crowns.'

'I prefer your offer, my lord, if I am bound to one.'

'You refuse?'

'Of course.'

'I told Michael you would;' and the villain, his temper restored, gave me the sunniest of smiles. 'The fact is, between ourselves,' he continued. 'Michael doesn't understand a gentleman.'

I began to laugh.

'And you?' I asked.

'I do,' he said. 'Well, well, the halter be it.'

'I'm sorry you won't live to see it,' I observed.

'Has his Majesty done me the honour to fasten a particular quarrel on me?'

'I would you were a few years older, though.'

'Oh, God gives years, but the devil gives increase,' laughed he. 'I can hold my own.'

'How is your prisoner?' I asked.

'The k——?'

'Your prisoner.'

'I forgot your wishes, sire. Well, he is alive.'

He rose to his feet; I imitated him. Then, with a smile, he said:

'And the pretty princess? Faith, I'll wager the next Elphberg will be red enough, for all that Black Michael will be called his father.'

I sprang a step towards him, clenching my hand. He did not move an inch, and his lip curled in insolent amusement.

'Go, while your skin's whole!' I muttered. He had repaid me with interest my hit about his mother.

Then came the most audacious thing I have known in my life. My friends were some thirty yards away. Rupert called to a groom to bring him his horse, and dismissed the fellow with a crown. The horse stood near. I stood still, suspecting nothing. Rupert made as though to mount; then he suddenly turned to me, his left hand resting in his belt, his right outstretched:

'Shake hands,' he said.

I bowed, and did as he had foreseen—I put my hands behind me. Quicker than thought, his left hand darted out at me, and a small dagger flashed in the air; he struck me in the left shoulder—had I not swerved, it had been my heart. With a cry, I staggered back. Without touching the stirrup, he leapt upon his horse and was off like an arrow, pursued by cries and revolver-shots—the last as useless as the first,—and I sank into my chair, bleeding profusely, as I watched the devil's brat disappear down the long avenue. My friends surrounded me, and then I fainted.

I suppose that I was put to bed, and there lay, unconscious, or half-conscious, for many hours; for it was night when I awoke to my full mind, and found Fritz beside me. I was weak and weary, but he bade me be of good cheer, saying that my wound would soon heal, and that meanwhile all had gone well, for Johann, the keeper, had fallen into the snare we had laid for him, and was even now in the house.

'And the queer thing is,' pursued Fritz, 'that I fancy he's not altogether sorry to find himself here. He seems to think that when Black Michael has brought off his *coup*, witnesses of how it was effected—saving, of course, the Six themselves—will not be at a premium.'

This idea argued a shrewdness in our captive which led me to build hopes on his assistance. I ordered him to be brought in at once. Sapt conducted him, and set him in a chair by my bedside. He was sullen and afraid; but, to say truth, after young Rupert's exploit, we also had our fears, and, if he got as far as possible from Sapt's formidable six-shooter, Sapt kept him as far as he could from me. Moreover, when he came in his hands were bound, but that I would not suffer.

I need not stay to recount the safeguards and rewards we promised the fellow—all of which were honourably observed and paid, so that he lives now in prosperity (though where I may not mention); and we were the more free inasmuch as we soon learnt that he was rather a weak man than a wicked, and had acted throughout this matter more from fear of the duke and of his own brother Max than for any love of what was done. But he had persuaded all of his loyalty; and though not in their secret counsels, was yet, by his knowledge of their dispositions within the Castle, able to lay bare before us the very heart of their devices. And here, in brief, is his story:

Below the level of the ground in the Castle, approached by a flight of stone steps which abutted on the end of the drawbridge, were situate two small rooms, cut out of the rock itself. The outer of the two had no windows, but was always lighted with candles; the inner had one square window, which gave upon the moat. In the outer room there lay always, day and night, three of the Six; and the instructions of Duke Michael were, that on any attack being made on the outer room, the three were to defend the door of it so long as they could without risk to themselves. But, so soon as the door should be in danger of being forced, then Rupert Hentzau or Detchard (for one of these two was always there) should leave the others to hold it as long as they could, and himself pass into the inner room, and, without more ado, kill the king who lay there, well-treated indeed, but without weapons, and with his arms confined in fine steel chains, which did not allow him to move his elbow more than three inches from his side. Thus, before the outer door were stormed, the king would be dead. And his body? For his body would be evidence as damning as himself.

'Nay, sir,' said Johann, 'his Highness has thought of that. While the two hold the outer room, the one who has killed the king unlocks the bars in the square window (they turn on a hinge). The window now gives no light, for its mouth is choked by a great pipe of earthenware; and this pipe, which is large enough to let pass through it the body of a man, passes into the moat, coming to an end immediately above the surface of the water, so that there is no perceptible interval between water and pipe. The king being dead, his murderer swiftly ties a weight to the body, and, dragging it to the window, raises it by a pulley (for, lest the weight should prove too great, Detchard has provided one) till it is level with the mouth of the pipe. He inserts the feet in the pipe, and pushes the body down. Silently, without splash or sound, it falls into the water and thence to the bottom of the moat, which is twenty feet deep thereabouts. This done, the murderer cries loudly, "All's well!" and himself slides down the pipe; and the others, if they can and the attack is not too hot, run to the inner room and, seeking a moment's delay, bar the door, and in their turn slide down. And though the king rises not from the bottom, they rise and swim round to the other side, where the orders are for men to wait them with ropes, to haul them out, and horses. And here, if things go ill, the duke will join them and seek safety by riding; but if all goes well, they will return to the Castle, and have their enemies in a trap. That, sir, is the plan of his Highness for the disposal of the king in case of need. But it is not to be used till the last; for, as we all know, he is not minded to kill the king unless he can, before or soon after, kill you also, sir. Now, sir, I have spoken the truth, as God is my witness, and I pray you to shield me from the vengeance of Duke Michael; for if, after he knows what I have done, I fall into his hands, I shall pray for one thing out of all the world—a speedy death, and that I shall not obtain from him!'

The fellow's story was rudely told, but our questions supplemented his narrative. What he had told us applied to an armed attack; but if suspicions were aroused, and there came overwhelming force—such, for instance, as I, the king, could bring—the idea of resistance would be abandoned; the king would be quietly murdered and slid down the pipe. And—here comes an ingenious touch—one of the Six would take his place in the cell, and, on the entrance of the searchers, loudly demand release and redress; and Michael, being summoned, would confess to hasty action, but he would say the man had angered him by seeking the favour of a lady in the Castle (this was Antoinette de Mauban), and he had confined him there, as he conceived he, as Lord of Zenda, had right to do. But he was now, on receiving his apology, content to let him go, and so end the gossip which, to his Highness's annoyance, had arisen concerning a prisoner in Zenda, and had given his visitors the trouble of this inquiry. The visitors, baffled, would retire, and Michael could, at his leisure, dispose of the body of the king.

Sapt, Fritz, and I in my bed, looked round on one another in horror and bewilderment at the cruelty and cunning of the plan. Whether I went in peace or in war, openly at the head of a *corps*,* or secretly by a stealthy assault, the king would be dead before I could come near him. If Michael were stronger and overcame my party, there would be an end. But if I were stronger, I should have no way to punish him, no means of proving any guilt in him without proving my own guilt also. On the other hand, I should be left as king (ah! for a moment my pulse quickened), and it would be for the future to witness the final struggle between him and me. He seemed to have made triumph possible and ruin impossible. At the worst, he would stand as well as he had stood before I crossed his path—with but one man between him and the throne, and that man an impostor; at best, there would be none left to stand against him. I had begun to think that Black Michael was over fond of leaving the fighting to his friends; but now I acknowledged that the brains, if not the arms, of the conspiracy were his.

'Does the king know this?' I asked.

'I and my brother,' answered Johann, 'put up the pipe, under the orders of my Lord of Hentzau. He was on guard that day, and the king asked my lord what it meant. "Faith," he answered, with his airy laugh, "it's a new improvement on the ladder of Jacob,* whereby, as you have read, sire, men pass from earth to heaven. We thought it not meet that your Majesty should go, in case, sire, you must go, by the common route. So we have made you a pretty private passage, where the vulgar cannot stare at you or incommode your passage. That, sire, is the meaning of that pipe." And he laughed and bowed, and prayed the king's leave to replenish the king's glass—for the king was at supper. And the king, though he is a brave man, as are all of his House, grew red and then white as he looked on the pipe and at the merry devil who mocked him. Ah, sir' (and the fellow shuddered), 'it is not easy to sleep quiet in the Castle of Zenda, for all of them would as soon cut a man's throat as play a game at cards; and my Lord Rupert would choose it sooner for a pastime than any other—ay, sooner than he would ruin a woman, though that he loves also.'

The man ceased, and I bade Fritz take him away and have him carefully guarded; and, turning to him, I added:

'If anyone asks you if there is a prisoner in Zenda, you may answer "Yes." But if any asks who the prisoner is, do not answer. For all my promises will not save you if any man here learns from you the truth as to the prisoner in Zenda. I'll kill you like a dog if the thing be so much as breathed within the house!'

Then, when he was gone, I looked at Sapt.

'It is a hard nut' said I.

'So hard,' said he, shaking his grizzled head, 'that, as I think, this time next year is like to find you still king of Ruritania!' and he broke out into curses on Michael's cunning.

I lay back on my pillows.

'There seem to me,' I observed, 'to be two ways by which the king can come out of Zenda alive. One is by treachery in the duke's followers.'

'You can leave that out,' said Sapt.

'I hope not,' I rejoined, 'because the other I was about to mention is—by a miracle from heaven!'

CHAPTER XIV

A NIGHT OUTSIDE THE CASTLE

It would have surprised the good people of Ruritania to know of the foregoing talk; for, according to the official reports, I had suffered a grievous and dangerous hurt from an accidental spear-thrust, received in the course of my sport. I caused the bulletins to be of a very serious character, and created great public excitement, whereby three things occurred: first, I gravely offended the medical faculty of Strelsau by refusing to summon to my bedside any of them, save a young man, a friend of Fritz's, whom we could trust; secondly, I received word from Marshal Strakencz that my orders seemed to have no more weight than his, and that the Princess Flavia was leaving for Tarlenheim under his unwilling escort (news whereat I strove not to be glad and proud); and thirdly, my brother, the Duke of Strelsau, although too well informed to believe the account of the origin of my sickness, was yet persuaded by the reports and by my seeming inactivity that I was in truth incapable of action, and that my life was in some danger. This I learnt from the man Johann, whom I was compelled to trust and send back to Zenda, where, by the way, Rupert Hentzau had him soundly flogged for daring to smirch the morals of Zenda by staying out all night in the pursuits of love. This, from Rupert, Johann deeply resented, and the duke's approval of it did more to bind the keeper to my side than all my promises.

On Flavia's arrival I cannot dwell. Her joy at finding me up and well, instead of on my back and fighting with death, makes a picture that even now dances before my eyes till they grow too dim to see it; and her reproaches that I had not trusted even her, must excuse the means I took to quiet them. In truth, to have her with me once more was like a taste of heaven to a damned soul, the sweeter for the inevitable doom that was to follow; and I rejoiced in being able to waste two whole days with her. And when I had wasted two days, the Duke of Strelsau arranged a hunting-party.

The stroke was near now. For Sapt and I, after anxious consultations, had resolved that we must risk a blow, our resolution being clinched* by Johann's news that the king grew peaked, pale, and ill, and that his health was breaking down under his rigorous confinement. Now a man—be he king or no king—may as well die swiftly and as becomes a gentleman, from bullet or thrust, as rot his life out in a cellar! That thought made prompt action advisable in the interests of the king; from my own point of view, it grew more and more necessary. For Strakencz urged on me the need of a speedy marriage, and my own inclinations seconded him with such terrible insistence that I feared for my resolution. I do not believe that I should have done the deed I dreamt of; but I might have come to flight, and my flight would have ruined the cause. And—yes, I am no saint (ask my little sister-in-law), and worse still might have happened.

It is perhaps as strange a thing as has ever been in the history of a country that the king's brother and the king's personator, in a time of profound outward peace, near a placid undisturbed country town, under semblance of amity, should wage a desperate war for the person and life of the king. Yet such was the struggle that began now between Zenda and Tarlenheim. When I look back on the time, I seem to myself to have been half-mad. Sapt has told me that I suffered no interference and listened to no remonstrances; and if ever a King of Ruritania ruled like a despot, I was, in those days, the man. Look where I would, I saw nothing that made life sweet to me, and I took my life in my hand and carried it carelessly as a man dangles an old glove. At first they strove to guard me, to keep me safe, to persuade me not to expose myself; but when they saw how I was set, there grew up among them—whether they knew the truth or not—a feeling that Fate ruled the issue, and that I must be left to play my game with Michael my own way.

Late next night I rose from table, where Flavia had sat by me, and conducted her to the door of her apartments. There I kissed her hand, and bade her sleep sound and wake to happy days. Then I changed my clothes and went out. Sapt and Fritz were waiting for me with six men and the horses. Over his saddle Sapt carried a long coil of rope, and both were heavily armed. I had with me a short stout cudgel and a long knife. Making a circuit, we avoided the town, and in an hour found ourselves slowly mounting the hill that led to the Castle of Zenda. The night was dark and very stormy; gusts of wind and spits of rain caught us as we breasted the incline, and the great trees moaned and sighed. When we came to a thick clump, about a quarter of a mile from the Castle, we bade our six friends hide there with the horses. Sapt had a whistle, and they could rejoin us in a few moments, if danger came: but, up till now, we had met no one. I hoped that Michael was still off his guard, believing me to be safe in bed. However that might be, we gained the top of the hill without accident, and found ourselves on the edge of the moat where it sweeps under the road, separating the old Castle from it. A tree stood on the edge of the bank, and Sapt, silently and diligently, set to make fast the rope. I stripped off my boots, took a pull at a flask of brandy, loosened the knife in its sheath, and took the cudgel between my teeth. Then I shook hands with my friends, not heeding a last look of entreaty from Fritz, and laid hold of the rope. I was going to have a look at Jacob's Ladder.

Gently I lowered myself into the water. Though the night was wild, the day had been warm and bright, and the water was not cold. I struck out, and began to swim round the great walls which frowned above me. I could see only three yards ahead; I had then good hopes of not being seen, as I crept along close under the damp, moss-grown masonry. There were lights from the new part of the Castle on the other side, and now and again I heard laughter and merry shouts. I fancied I recognised young Rupert Hentzau's ringing tones, and pictured him flushed with wine. Recalling my thoughts to the business in hand, I rested a moment. If Johann's description were right, I must be near the window now. Very slowly I moved; and, out of the darkness ahead, loomed a shape. It was the pipe, curving from the window to the water: about four feet of its surface were displayed; it was as big round as two men. I was about to approach it, when I saw something else, and my heart stood still. The nose of a boat protruded beyond the pipe on the other side; and listening intently, I heard a slight shuffle—as of a man shifting his position. Who was the man who guarded Michael's invention? Was he awake or was he asleep? I felt if my knife were ready, and trod water; as I did so, I found bottom under my feet. The foundations of the Castle extended some fifteen inches, making a ledge; and I stood on it, out of water from my armpits upwards. Then I crouched and peered through the darkness under the pipe, where, curving, it left a space.

There was a man in the boat. A rifle lay by him—I saw the gleam of the barrel. Here was the sentinel! He sat very still. I listened: he breathed heavily, regularly, monotonously. By heaven, he slept! Kneeling on the shelf, I drew forward under the pipe till my face was within two feet of his. He was a big man, I saw. It was Max Holf, the brother of Johann. My hand stole to my belt, and I drew out my knife. Of all the deeds of my life, I love the least to think of this, and whether it were the act of a man or a traitor I will not ask. I said to myself: 'It is war—and the king's life is the stake.' And I raised myself from beneath the pipe and stood up by the boat, which lay moored by the ledge. Holding my breath, I marked the spot and raised my arm. The great fellow stirred. He opened his eyes—wide, wider. He gasped in terror at my face and clutched at his rifle. I struck home. And I heard the chorus of a love-song from the opposite bank.

Leaving him where he lay, a huddled mass, I turned to 'Jacob's Ladder'. My time was short. This fellow's turn of watching might be over directly, and relief would come. Leaning over the pipe, I examined it, from the end near the water to the topmost extremity where it passed, or seemed to pass, through the masonry of the wall. There was no break in it, no chink. Dropping on my knees, I tested the under side. And my breath went quick and fast, for on this lower side, where the pipe should have clung close to the masonry, there was a gleam of light! That light must come from the cell of the king! I set my shoulder against the pipe and exerted my strength. The chink widened a very, very little, and hastily I desisted; I had done enough to show that the pipe was not fixed in the masonry at the lower side.

Then I heard a voice—a harsh, grating voice:

'Well, sire, if you have had enough of my society, I will leave you to repose; but I must fasten the little ornaments first.'

It was Detchard! I caught the English accent in a moment.

'Have you anything to ask, sire, before we part?'

The king's voice followed. It was his, though it was faint and hollow—different from the merry tones I had heard in the glades of the forest.

'Pray my brother,' said the king, 'to kill me. I am dying by inches here.'

'The duke does not desire your death, sire—yet,' sneered Detchard; 'when he does, behold your path to heaven!'

The king answered:

'So be it! And now, if your orders allow it, pray leave me.'

'May you dream of paradise!' said the ruffian.

The light disappeared. I heard the bolts of the door run home. And then I heard the sobs of the king. He was alone, as he thought. Who dares mock at him?

I did not venture to speak to him. The risk of some exclamation escaping him in surprise was too great. I dared do nothing that night; and my task now was to get myself away in safety, and to carry off the carcase of the dead man. To leave him there would tell too much. Casting loose the boat, I got in. The wind was blowing a gale now, and there was little danger of oars being heard. I rowed swiftly round to where my friends waited. I had just reached the spot, when a loud whistle sounded over the moat behind me.

'Hullo, Max!' I heard shouted.

I hailed Sapt in a low tone. The rope came down. I tied it round the corpse, and then went up it myself.

'Whistle you too,' I whispered, 'for our men, and haul in the line. No talk now.'

They hauled up the body. Just as it reached the road, three men on horseback swept round from the front of the Castle. We saw them; but, being on foot ourselves, we escaped their notice. But we heard our men coming up with a shout.

'The devil, but it's dark!' cried a ringing voice.

It was young Rupert. A moment later, shots rang out. Our people had met them. I started forward at a run, Sapt and Fritz following me.

'Thrust, thrust!' cried Rupert again, and a loud groan following told that he himself was not behindhand.

'I'm done, Rupert!' cried a voice. 'They're two to one. Save yourself!'

I ran on, holding my cudgel in my hand. Suddenly a horse came towards me. A man was on it, leaning over his shoulder.

'Are you cooked* too, Krafstein?' he cried.

There was no answer.

I sprang to the horse's head. It was Rupert Hentzau.

'At last!' I cried.

For we seemed to have him. He had only his sword in his hand. My men were hot upon him; Sapt and Fritz were running up. I had outstripped them; but if they got close enough to fire, he must die or surrender.

'At last!' I cried.

'It's the play-actor!' cried he, slashing at my cudgel. He cut it clean in two; and, judging discretion better than death, I ducked my head and (I blush to tell it) scampered for my life. The devil was in Rupert Hentzau; for he put spurs to his horse, and I, turning to look, saw him ride, full gallop, to the edge of the moat and leap in, while the shots of our party fell thick round him like hail. With one gleam of moonlight we should have riddled him with balls; but, in the darkness, he won to the corner of the Castle, and vanished from our sight.

'The deuce take him!' grinned Sapt.

'It's a pity,' said I, 'that he's a villain. Whom have we got?'

We had Lauengram and Krafstein: they lay dead; and concealment being no longer possible, we flung them, with Max, into the moat; and, drawing together in a compact body, rode off down the hill. And, in our midst, went the bodies of three gallant gentlemen. Thus we travelled home, heavy at heart for the death of our friends, sore uneasy concerning the king, and cut to the quick that young Rupert had played yet another winning hand with us.

For my own part, I was vexed and angry that I had killed no man in open fight, but only stabbed a knave in his sleep. And I did not love to hear Rupert call me a play-actor.

CHAPTER XV

I TALK WITH A TEMPTER

RURITANIA is not England, or the quarrel between Duke Michael and myself could not have gone on, with the remarkable incidents which marked it, without more public notice being directed to it. Duels were frequent among all the upper classes, and private quarrels between great men kept the old habit of spreading to their friends and dependants. Nevertheless, after the affray which I have just related, such reports began to circulate that I felt it necessary to be on my guard. The death of the gentlemen involved could not be hidden from their relatives. I issued a stern order, declaring that duelling had attained unprecedented licence (the Chancellor drew up the document for me, and very well he did it), and forbidding it save in the gravest cases. I sent a public and stately apology to Michael, and he returned a deferential and courteous reply to me; for our one point of union was—and it underlay all our differences and induced an unwilling harmony between our actions—that we could neither of us afford to throw our cards on the table. He, as well as I, was a 'play-actor', and, hating one another, we combined to dupe public opinion. Unfortunately, however, the necessity for concealment involved the necessity of delay: the king might die in his prison, or even be spirited off somewhere else; it could not be helped. For a little while I was compelled to observe a truce, and my only consolation was that Flavia most warmly approved of my edict against duelling; and, when I expressed delight at having won her favour, prayed me, if her favour were any motive to me, to prohibit the practice altogether.

'Wait till we are married,' said I, smiling.

Not the least peculiar result of the truce and of the secrecy which dictated it was that the town of Zenda became in the daytime—I would not have trusted far to its protection by night—a sort of neutral zone, where both parties could safely go; and I, riding down one day with Flavia and Sapt, had an encounter with an acquaintance, which presented a ludicrous side, but was at the same time embarrassing. As I rode along, I met a dignified-looking person driving in a two-horsed carriage. He stopped his horses, got out, and approached me, bowing low. I recognised the Head of the Strelsau Police.

'Your Majesty's ordinance as to duelling is receiving our best attention,' he assured me.

If the best attention involved his presence in Zenda, I determined at once to dispense with it.

'Is that what brings you to Zenda, Prefect?' I asked.

'Why no, sire; I am here because I desired to oblige the British Ambassador.'

'What's the British Ambassador doing *dans cette galère?*'* said I, carelessly.

'A young countryman of his, sire—a man of some position,—is missing. His friends have not heard from him for two months, and there is reason to believe that he was last seen in Zenda.'

Flavia was paying little attention. I dared not look at Sapt.

'What reason?'

'A friend of his in Paris—a certain M. Featherly—has given us information which makes it possible that he came here, and the officials of the railway recollect his name on some luggage.'

'What was his name?'

'Rassendyll, sire,' he answered; and I saw that the name meant nothing to him. But, glancing at Flavia, he lowered his voice as he went on: 'It is thought that he may have followed a lady here. Has your Majesty heard of a certain Madame de Mauban?'

'Why, yes,' said I, my eye involuntarily travelling towards the Castle.

'She arrived in Ruritania about the same time as this Rassendyll.'

I caught the Prefect's glance; he was regarding me with inquiry writ large on his face.

'Sapt,' said I, 'I must speak a word to the Prefect. Will you ride on a few paces with the princess?' And I added to the Prefect: 'Come, sir, what do you mean?'

He drew close to me, and I bent in the saddle.

'If he were in love with the lady?' he whispered. 'Nothing has been heard of him for two months;' and this time it was the eye of the Prefect which travelled towards the Castle.

'Yes, the lady is there,' I said quietly. 'But I don't suppose Mr. Rassendyll—is that the name?—is.'

'The duke,' he whispered, 'does not like rivals, sire.'

'You're right there,' said I, with all sincerity. 'But surely you hint at a very grave charge?'

He spread his hands out in apology. I whispered in his ear:

'This is a grave matter. Go back to Strelsau——'

'But, sire, if I have a clue here?'

'Go back to Strelsau,' I repeated. 'Tell the Ambassador that you have a clue, but that you must be left alone for a week or two. Meanwhile, I'll charge myself with looking into the matter.'

'The Ambassador is very pressing, sire.'

'You must quiet him. Come, sir; you see that if your suspicions are correct, it is an affair in which we must move with caution. We can have no scandal. Mind you return tonight.'

He promised to obey me, and I rode on to rejoin my companions, a little easier in my mind. Inquiries after me must be stopped at all hazards for a week or two; and this clever official had come surprisingly near the truth. His impression might be useful some day, but if he acted on it now it might mean the worst to the king. Heartily did I curse George Featherly for not holding his tongue.

'Well,' asked Flavia, 'have you finished your business?'

'Most satisfactorily,' said I. 'Come, shall we turn round? We are almost trenching on my brother's territory.'

We were, in fact, at the extreme end of the town, just where the hill begins to mount towards the Castle. We cast our eyes up, admiring the massive beauty of the old walls, and we saw a *cortège* winding slowly down the hill. On it came.

'Let us go back,' said Sapt.

'I should like to stay,' said Flavia; and I reined my horse beside hers.

We could distinguish the approaching party now. There came first two mounted servants in black uniforms, relieved only by a silver badge. These were followed by a car drawn by four horses: on it, under a heavy pall, lay a coffin; behind it rode a man in plain black clothes, carrying his hat in his hand. Sapt uncovered, and we stood waiting, Flavia keeping by me and laying her hand on my arm.

'It is one of the gentlemen killed in the quarrel, I expect,' she said.

I beckoned to a groom.

'Ride and ask whom they escort,' I ordered.

He rode up to the servants, and I saw him pass on to the gentleman who rode behind.

'It's Rupert of Hentzau,' whispered Sapt.

Rupert it was, and directly afterwards, waving to the procession to stand still, Rupert trotted up to me. He was in a frock-coat, tightly buttoned, and trousers. He wore an aspect of sadness, and he bowed with profound respect. Yet suddenly he smiled, and I smiled too, for old Sapt's hand lay in his left breast-pocket, and Rupert and I both guessed what lay in the hand inside the pocket.

'Your Majesty asks whom we escort,' said Rupert. 'It is my dear friend, Albert of Lauengram.'

'Sir,' said I, 'no one regrets the unfortunate affair more than I. My ordinance, which I mean to have obeyed, is witness to it.'

'Poor fellow!' said Flavia softly, and I saw Rupert's eyes flash at her. Whereat I grew red; for, if I had my way, Rupert Hentzau should not have defiled her by so much as a glance. Yet he did it and dared to let admiration be seen in his look.

'Your Majesty's words are gracious,' he said. 'I grieve for my friend. Yet, sire, others must soon lie as he lies now.'

'It is a thing we all do well to remember, my lord,' I rejoined.

'Even kings, sire,' said Rupert, in a moralising tone; and old Sapt swore softly by my side.

'It is true,' said I. 'How fares my brother, my lord?'

'He is better, sire.'

'I am rejoiced.'

'He hopes soon to leave for Strelsau, when his health is secured.'

'He is only convalescent, then?'

'There remain one or two small troubles,' answered the insolent fellow, in the mildest tone in the world.

'Express my earnest hope,' said Flavia, 'that they may soon cease to trouble him.'

'Your Royal Highness's wish is, humbly, my own,' said Rupert, with a bold glance that brought a blush to Flavia's cheek.

I bowed; and Rupert, bowing lower, backed his horse and signed to his party to proceed. With a sudden impulse, I rode after him. He turned swiftly, fearing that, even in the presence of the dead and before a lady's eyes, I meant him mischief.

'You fought as a brave man the other night,' I said. 'Come, you are young, sir. If you will deliver your prisoner alive to me, you shall come to no hurt.'

He looked at me with a mocking smile; but suddenly he rode nearer to me.

'I'm unarmed,' he said; 'and our old Sapt there could pick me off in a minute.'

'I'm not afraid,' said I.

'No, curse you!' he answered. 'Look here, I made you a proposal from the duke once.'

'I'll hear nothing from Black Michael,' said I.

'Then hear one from me.' He lowered his voice to a whisper. 'Attack the Castle boldly. Let Sapt and Tarlenheim lead.'

'Go on,' said I.

'Arrange the time with me.'

'I have such confidence in you, my lord!'

'Tut! I'm talking business now. Sapt there and Fritz will fall; Black Michael will fall——'

'What!'

'——Black Michael will fall, like the dog he is; the prisoner, as you call him, will go by Jacob's Ladder—ah, you know that!—to hell! Two men will be left—I, Rupert Hentzau, and you, the King of Ruritania.'

He paused, and then, in a voice that quivered with eagerness, added:

'Isn't that a hand to play?—a throne and your princess! And for me, say a competence and your Majesty's gratitude.'

'Surely,' I exclaimed, 'while you're above ground, hell wants its master!'

'Well, think it over,' he said. 'And, look you, it would take more than a scruple or two to keep me from yonder girl,' and his eye flashed again at her I loved.

'Get out of my reach!' said I; and yet in a moment I began to laugh for the very audacity of it.

'Would you turn against your master?' I asked.

He swore at Michael for being what the offspring of a legal, though morganatic, union should not be called, and said to me, in an almost confidential and apparently friendly tone:

'He gets in my way, you know. He's a jealous brute! Faith, I nearly stuck a knife into him last night; he came most cursedly *mal à propos!*'*

My temper was well under control now: I was learning something.

'A lady?' I asked negligently.

'Ay, and a beauty,' he nodded. 'But you've seen her.'

'Ah! was it at a tea-party, when some of your friends got on the wrong side of the table?'

'What can you expect of fools like Detchard and De Gautet? I wish I'd been there.'

'And the duke interferes?'

'Well,' said Rupert meditatively, 'that's hardly a fair way of putting it, perhaps. I want to interfere.'

'And she prefers the duke?'

'Ay, the silly creature! Ah, well, you think about my plan;' and, with a bow, he pricked his horse and trotted after the body of his friend.

I went back to Flavia and Sapt, pondering on the strangeness of the man. Wicked men I have known in plenty, but Rupert Hentzau remains unique in my experience. And if there be another anywhere, let him be caught and hanged out of hand. So say I!

'He's very handsome, isn't he?' said Flavia.

Well, of course she didn't know him as I did; yet I was put out, for I thought his bold glances would have made her angry. But my dear Flavia was a woman, and so—she was not put out. On the contrary, she thought young Rupert very handsome—as, beyond question, the ruffian was.

'And how sad he looked at his friend's death!' said she.

'He'll have better reason to be sad at his own,' observed Sapt, with a grim smile.

As for me, I grew sulky; unreasonable it was perhaps, for what better business had I to look at her with love than had even Rupert's lustful eyes? And sulky I remained till, as evening fell and we rode up to Tarlenheim, Sapt having fallen behind in case anyone should be following us, Flavia, riding close beside me, said softly, with a little half-ashamed laugh:

'Unless you smile, Rudolf, I cry. Why are you angry?'

'It was something that fellow said to me,' said I; but I was smiling as we reached the doors and dismounted.

There a servant handed me a note; it was unaddressed.

'Is it for me?' I asked.

'Yes, sire; a boy brought it.'

I tore it open:

'*Johann carries this for me. I warned you once. In the name of God, and if you are a man, rescue me from this den of murderers!—A. de M.*'

I handed it to Sapt; but all that the tough old soul said in reply to this piteous appeal was:

'Whose fault brought her there?'

Nevertheless, not being faultless myself, I took leave to pity Antoinette de Mauban.

CHAPTER XVI

A DESPERATE PLAN

As I had ridden publicly in Zenda, and had talked there with Rupert Hentzau, of course all pretence of illness was at an end. I marked the effect on the garrison of Zenda: they ceased to be seen abroad; and any of my men who went near the Castle reported that the utmost vigilance prevailed there. Touched as I was by Madame de Mauban's appeal, I seemed as powerless to befriend her as I had proved to help the king. Michael bade me defiance; and—although he too had been seen outside the walls—with more disregard for appearances than he had hitherto shown, he did not take the trouble to send any excuse for his failure to wait on the king. Time ran on in inactivity, when every moment was pressing; for not only was I faced with the new danger which the stir about my own disappearance brought on me, but great murmurs had arisen in Strelsau at my continued absence from the city. They had been greater, but for the knowledge that Flavia was with me; and for this reason I suffered her to stay, though I hated to have her where danger was, and though every day of our present sweet intercourse strained my endurance almost to breaking. As a final blow, nothing would content my advisers, Strakencz and the Chancellor (who came out from Strelsau to make an urgent representation to me) save that I should appoint a day for the public solemnisation of my betrothal, a ceremony which in Ruritania is well-nigh as binding and great a thing as the marriage itself. And this—with Flavia sitting by me—I was forced to do, setting a date a fortnight ahead, and appointing the Cathedral in Strelsau as the place. And this formal act being published far and wide, caused great joy throughout the kingdom, and was the talk of all tongues: so that I reckoned there were but two men who chafed at it—I mean Black Michael and myself; and but one who did not know of it—that one the man whose name I bore, the King of Ruritania.

In truth, I heard something of the way the news was received in the Castle; for after an interval of three days, the man Johann, greedy for more money, though fearful for his life, again found means to visit us.

He had been waiting on the duke when the tidings came. Black Michael's face had grown blacker still, and he had sworn savagely; nor was he better pleased when young Rupert took oath that I meant to do as I said, and turning to Madame de Mauban, wished her joy on a rival gone. Michael's hand stole towards his sword (said Johann), but not a bit did Rupert care; for he rallied the duke on having made a better king than had reigned for years past in Ruritania. 'And,' said he, with a meaning bow to his exasperated master, 'the devil sends the princess a finer man than heaven had marked out for her, by my soul, it does!' Then Michael harshly bade him hold his tongue, and leave them; but Rupert must needs first kiss madame's hand, which he did as though he loved her, while Michael glared at him.

This was the lighter side of the fellow's news; but more serious came behind, and it was plain that if time pressed at Tarlenheim, it pressed none the less fiercely at Zenda. For the king was very sick: Johann had seen him, and he was wasted and hardly able to move. 'There could be no thought of taking another for him now.' So alarmed were they, that they had sent for a physician from Strelsau; and the physician having been introduced into the king's cell, had come forth pale and trembling, and urgently prayed the duke to let him go back and meddle no more in the affair; but the duke would not, and held him there a prisoner, telling him his life was safe if the king lived while the duke desired and died when the duke desired—not otherwise. And, persuaded by the physician, they had allowed Madame de Mauban to visit the king and give him such attendance as his state needed, and as only a woman can give. Yet his life hung in the balance; and I was still strong and whole and free. Wherefore great gloom reigned at Zenda; and save when they quarrelled, to which they were very prone, they hardly spoke. But the deeper the depression of the rest, young Rupert went about Satan's work with a smile in his eye and a song on his lip; and laughed 'fit to burst' (said Johann) because the duke always set Detchard to guard the king when Madame de Mauban was in the cell—which precaution was, indeed, not unwise in my careful brother. Thus Johann told his tale and seized his crowns. Yet he besought us to allow him to stay with us in Tarlenheim, and not venture his head again in the lion's den; but we had need of him there, and, although I refused to constrain him, I prevailed on him by increased rewards to go back and to carry tidings to Madame de Mauban that I was working for her, and that, if she could, she should speak one word of comfort to the king. For while suspense is bad for the sick, yet despair is worse still, and it might be that the king lay dying of mere hopelessness, for I could learn of no definite disease that afflicted him.

'And how do they guard the king now?' I asked, remembering that two of the Six were dead, and Max Holf also.

'Detchard and Bersonin watch by night, Rupert Hentzau and De Gautet by day, sir,' he answered.

'Only two at a time?'

'Ay, sir; but the others rest in a room just above, and are within sound of a cry or a whistle.'

'A room just above? I didn't know of that. Is there any communication between it and the room where they watch?'

'No, sir. You must go down a few stairs and through the door by the drawbridge, and so to where the king is lodged.'

'And that door is locked?'

'Only the four lords have keys, sir.'

I drew nearer to him.

'And have they keys of the grating?' I asked in a low whisper.

'I think, sir, only Detchard and Rupert.'

'Where does the duke lodge?'

'In the *château*, on the first floor. His apartments are on the right as you go towards the drawbridge.'

'And Madame de Mauban?'

'Just opposite, on the left. But her door is locked after she has entered.'

'To keep her in?'

'Doubtless, sir.'

'Perhaps for another reason?'

'It is possible.'

'And the duke, I suppose, has the key?'

'Yes. And the drawbridge is drawn back at night, and of that too the duke holds the key, so that it cannot be run across the moat without application to him.'

'And where do you sleep?'

'In the entrance-hall of the *château*, with five servants.'

'Armed?'

'They have pikes, sir, but no firearms. The duke will not trust them with firearms.'

Then at last I took the matter boldly in my hands. I had failed once at Jacob's Ladder; I should fail again there. I must make the attack from the other side.

'I have promised you twenty thousand crowns,' said I. 'You shall have fifty thousand if you will do what I ask of you tomorrow night. But, first, do those servants know who your prisoner is?'

'No, sir. They believe him to be some private enemy of the duke's.'

'And they would not doubt that I am the king?'

'How should they?' he asked.

'Look to this, then. Tomorrow, at two in the morning exactly, fling open the front door of the *château*. Don't fail by an instant.'

'Shall you be there, sir?'

'Ask no questions. Do what I tell you. Say the hall is close, or what you will. That is all I ask of you.'

'And may I escape by the door, sir, when I have opened it?'

'Yes, as quick as your legs will carry you. One thing more. Carry this note to madame—oh, it's in French, you can't read it—and charge her, for the sake of all our lives, not to fail in what it orders.'

The man was trembling, but I had to trust to what he had of courage and to what he had of honesty. I dared not wait, for I feared that the king would die.

When the fellow was gone, I called Sapt and Fritz to me, and unfolded the plan that I had formed. Sapt shook his head over it.

'Why can't you wait?' he asked.

'The king may die.'

'Michael will be forced to act before that.'

'Then,' said I, 'the king may live.'

'Well, and if he does?'

'For a fortnight?' I asked simply.

And Sapt bit his moustache.

Suddenly Fritz von Tarlenheim laid his hand on my shoulder.

'Let us go and make the attempt,' said he.

'I mean you to go—don't be afraid,' said I.

'Ay, but do you stay here, and take care of the princess.'

A gleam came into old Sapt's eye.

'We should have Michael one way or the other then,' he chuckled; 'whereas if you go, and are killed with the king, what will become of those of us who are left?'

'They will serve Queen Flavia,' said I, 'and I would to God I could be one of them.'

A pause followed. Old Sapt broke it by saying sadly, yet with an unmeant drollery that set Fritz and me laughing:

'Why didn't old Rudolf the Third marry your—great-grandmother, was it?'

'Come,' said I, 'it is the king we are thinking about.'

'It is true,' said Fritz.

'Moreover,' I went on, 'I have been an impostor for the profit of another, but I will not be one for my own; and if the king is not alive and on his throne before the day of betrothal comes, I will tell the truth, come what may.'

'You shall go, lad,' said Sapt.

Here is the plan I had made. A strong party under Sapt's command was to steal up to the door of the *château*. If discovered prematurely, they were to kill anyone who found them—with their swords, for I wanted no noise of firing. If all went well, they would be at the door when Johann opened it. They were to rush in and secure the servants if their mere presence and the use of the king's name were not enough. At the same moment—and on this hinged the plan—a woman's cry was to ring out loud and shrill from Antoinette de Mauban's chamber. Again and again she was to cry: 'Help, help! Michael, help!' and then to utter the name of young Rupert Hentzau. Then, as we hoped, Michael, in fury, would rush out of his apartments opposite, and fall alive into the hands of Sapt. Still the cries would go on; my men would let down the drawbridge; and it would be strange if Rupert, hearing his name thus taken in vain, did not descend from where he slept and seek to cross. De Gautet might or might not come with him: that must be left to chance.

And when Rupert set his foot on the drawbridge? There was my part: for I was minded for another swim in the moat; and, lest I should grow weary, I had resolved to take with me a small wooden ladder, on which I could rest my arms in the water—and my feet when I left it. I would rear it against the wall just by the bridge; and when the bridge was across, I would stealthily creep on to it—and then if Rupert or De Gautet crossed in safety, it would be my misfortune, not my fault. They dead, two men only would remain; and for them we must trust to the confusion we had created and to a sudden rush. We should have the keys of the door that led to the all-important rooms. Perhaps they would rush out. If they stood by their orders, then the king's life hung on the swiftness with which we could force the outer door; and I thanked God that not Rupert Hentzau watched, but Detchard. For though Detchard was a cool man, relentless, and no coward, he had neither the dash nor the recklessness of Rupert. Moreover, he, if any one of them, really loved Black Michael, and it might be that he would leave Bersonin to guard the king and rush across the bridge to take part in the affray on the other side.

So I planned—desperately. And, that our enemy might be the better lulled to security, I gave orders that our residence should be brilliantly lighted from top to bottom, as though we were engaged in revelry; and should so be kept all night, with music playing and people moving to and fro. Strakencz would be there, and he was to conceal our departure, if he could, from Flavia. And if we came not again by the morning, he was to march, openly and in force to the Castle, and demand the person of the king: if Black Michael were not there, as I did not think he would be, the marshal would take Flavia with him, as swiftly as he could, to Strelsau, and there proclaim Black Michael's treachery and the probable death of the king, and rally all that there was honest and true round the banner of the princess. And, to say truth, this was what I thought most likely to happen. For I had great doubts whether either the king or Black Michael or I had more than a day to live. Well, if Black Michael died, and if I, the play-actor, slew Rupert Hentzau with my own hand, and then died myself, it might be that Fate would deal as lightly with Ruritania as could be hoped, notwithstanding that she demanded the life of the king—and to her dealing thus with me, I was in no temper to make objection.

It was late when we rose from conference, and I betook me to the princess's apartments. She was pensive that evening; yet, when I left her, she flung her arms about me and grew, for an instant, bashfully radiant as she slipped a ring on my finger. I was wearing the king's ring; but I had also on my little finger a plain band of gold engraved with the motto of our family, '*Nil Quae Feci*'.* This I took off and put on her, and signed to her to let me go. And she, understanding, stood away and watched me with dimmed eyes.

'Wear that ring, even though you wear another when you are queen,' I said.

'Whatever else I wear, this I will wear till I die and after,' said she, as she kissed the ring.

CHAPTER XVII

YOUNG RUPERT'S MIDNIGHT DIVERSIONS

THE night came fine and clear. I had prayed for dirty weather, such as had favoured my previous voyage in the moat, but Fortune was this time against me. Still I reckoned that by keeping close under the wall and in the shadow I could escape detection from the windows of the *château* that looked out on the scene of my efforts. If they searched the moat, indeed, my scheme must fail; but I did not think they would. They had made Jacob's Ladder secure against attack. Johann had himself helped to fix it closely to the masonry on the under side, so that it could not now be moved from below any more than from above. An assault with explosives or a long battering with picks alone could displace it, and the noise involved in either of these operations put them out of the question. What harm, then, could a man do in the moat? I trusted that Black Michael, putting this query to himself, would answer confidently, 'None'; while, even if Johann meant treachery, he did not know my scheme, and would doubtless expect to see me, at the head of my friends, before the front entrance to the *château*. There, I said to Sapt, was the real danger.

'And there,' I added, 'you shall be. Doesn't that content you?'

But it did not. Dearly would he have liked to come with me, had I not utterly refused to take him. One man might escape notice, to double the party more than doubled the risk; and when he ventured to hint once again that my life was too valuable, I, knowing the secret thought he clung to, sternly bade him be silent, assuring him that unless the king lived through the night, I would not live through it either.

At twelve o'clock, Sapt's command left the *château* of Tarlenheim and struck off to the right, riding by unfrequented roads, and avoiding the town of Zenda. If all went well, they would be in front of the Castle by about a quarter to two. Leaving their horses half a mile off, they were to steal up to the entrance and hold themselves in readiness for the opening of the door. If the door were not opened by two, they were to send Fritz von Tarlenheim round to the other side of the

Castle. I would meet him there if I were alive, and we would consult whether to storm the Castle or not. If I were not there, they were to return with all speed to Tarlenheim, rouse the Marshal, and march in force on Zenda. For if not there, I should be dead; and I knew that the king would not be alive five minutes after I had ceased to breathe.

I must now leave Sapt and his friends, and relate how I myself proceeded on this eventful night. I went out on the good horse which had carried me, on the night of the coronation, back from the shooting-lodge to Strelsau. I carried a revolver in the saddle and my sword. I was covered with a large cloak, and under this I wore a warm, tight-fitting woollen jersey, a pair of knickerbockers, thick stockings, and light canvas shoes. I had rubbed myself thoroughly with oil, and I carried a large flask of whisky. The night was warm, but I might probably be immersed a long while, and it was necessary to take every precaution against cold: for cold not only saps a man's courage if he has to die, but impairs his energy if others have to die, and, finally, gives him rheumatics, if it be God's will that he live. Also I tied round my body a length of thin but stout cord, and I did not forget my ladder. I, starting after Sapt, took a shorter route, skirting the town to the left, and found myself in the outskirts of the forest at about half-past twelve. I tied my horse up in a thick clump of trees, leaving the revolver in its pocket in the saddle—it would be no use to me,—and, ladder in hand, made my way to the edge of the moat. Here I unwound my rope from about my waist, bound it securely round the trunk of a tree on the bank, and let myself down. The Castle clock struck a quarter to one as I felt the water under me and began to swim round the keep, pushing the ladder before me, and hugging the Castle wall. Thus voyaging, I came to my old friend, 'Jacob's Ladder', and felt the ledge of masonry under me. I crouched down in the shadow of the great pipe—I tried to stir it, but it was quite immovable—and waited. I remember that my predominant feeling was, neither anxiety for the king nor longing for Flavia, but an intense desire to smoke; and this craving, of course, I could not gratify.

The drawbridge was still in its place. I saw its airy, slight framework above me, some ten yards to my right, as I crouched with my back against the wall of the king's cell. I made out a window two yards my side of it and nearly on the same level. That, if Johann spoke true, must belong to the duke's apartments; and on the other side, in about the same relative position, must be Madame de Mauban's window. Women are careless, forgetful creatures. I prayed that she might not forget that she was to be the victim of a brutal attempt at two o'clock precisely. I was rather amused at the part I had assigned to my young friend Rupert Hentzau; but I owed him a stroke,—for, even as I sat, my shoulder ached where he had, with an audacity that seemed half to hide his treachery, struck at me, in sight of all my friends, on the terrace at Tarlenheim.

Suddenly the duke's window grew bright. The shutters were not closed, and the interior became partially visible to me as I cautiously raised myself till I stood on tiptoe. Thus placed, my range of sight embraced a yard or more inside the window, while the radius of light did not reach me. The window was flung open and someone looked out. I marked Antoinette de Mauban's graceful figure, and, though her face was in shadow, the fine outline of her head was revealed against the light behind. I longed to cry softly, 'Remember!' but I dared not—and happily, for a moment later a man came up and stood by her. He tried to put his arm round her waist, but with a swift motion she sprang away and leant against the shutter, her profile towards me. I made out who the new-comer was: it was young Rupert. A low laugh from him made me sure, as he leant forwards, stretching out his hand towards her.

'Gently, gently!' I murmured. 'You're too soon, my boy!'

His head was close to hers. I suppose he whispered to her, for I saw her point to the moat, and I heard her say, in slow and distinct tones:

'I had rather throw myself out of this window!'

He came close up to the window and looked out.

'It looks cold,' said he. 'Come, Antoinette, are you serious?'

She made no answer, so far as I heard; and he, smiting his hand petulantly on the window-sill, went on, in the voice of some spoilt child:

'Hang Black Michael! Isn't the princess enough for him? Is he to have everything? What the devil do you see in Black Michael?'

'If I told him what you say——' she began.

'Well, tell him,' said Rupert, carelessly; and, catching her off her guard, he sprang forward and kissed her, laughing, and crying, 'There's something to tell him!'

If I had kept my revolver with me, I should have been very sorely tempted. Being spared the temptation, I merely added this new score to his account.

'Though, faith,' said Rupert, 'it's little he cares. He's mad about the princess, you know. He talks of nothing but cutting the play-actor's throat.'

Didn't he, indeed?

'And if I do it for him, what do you think he's promised me?'

The unhappy woman raised her hands above her head, in prayer or in despair.

'But I detest waiting,' said Rupert; and I saw that he was about to lay his hand on her again, when there was a noise of a door in the room opening, and a harsh voice cried:

'What are you doing here, sir?'

Rupert turned his back to the window, bowed low, and said, in his loud, merry tones:

'Apologising for your absence, sir. Could I leave the lady alone?'

The new-comer must be Black Michael. I saw him directly, as he advanced towards the window. He caught young Rupert by the arm.

'The moat would hold more than the king!' said he, with a significant gesture.

'Does your Highness threaten me?' asked Rupert.

'A threat is more warning than most men get from me.'

'Yet,' observed Rupert, 'Rudolf Rassendyll has been much threatened, and yet lives!'

'Am I in fault because my servants bungle?' asked Michael scornfully.

'Your Highness has run no risk of bungling!' sneered Rupert.

It was telling the duke that he shirked danger as plain as ever I have heard a man told. Black Michael had self-control. I daresay he scowled—it was a great regret to me that I could not see their faces better,—but his voice was even and calm, as he answered:

'Enough, enough! We mustn't quarrel, Rupert. Are Detchard and Bersonin at their posts?'

'They are, sir.'

'I need you no more.'

'Nay, I'm not oppressed with fatigue,' said Rupert.

'Pray, sir, leave us,' said Michael, more impatiently. 'In ten minutes the drawbridge will be drawn back, and I presume you have no wish to swim to your bed.'

Rupert's figure disappeared. I heard the door open and shut again. Michael and Antoinette de Mauban were left together. To my chagrin, the duke laid his hand on the window and closed it. He stood talking to Antoinette for a moment or two. She shook her head, and he turned impatiently away. She left the window. The door sounded again, and Black Michael closed the shutters.

'De Gautet, De Gautet, man!' sounded from the drawbridge. 'Unless you want a bath before your bed, come along!'

It was Rupert's voice, coming from the end of the drawbridge. A moment later he and De Gautet stepped out on the bridge. Rupert's arm was through De Gautet's, and in the middle of the bridge he detained his companion and leant over. I dropped beside the shelter of 'Jacob's Ladder'.

Then Master Rupert had a little sport. He took from De Gautet a bottle which he carried, and put it to his lips.

'Hardly a drop!' he cried discontentedly, and flung it in the moat.

It fell, as I judged from the sound and the circles on the water, within a yard of the pipe. And Rupert, taking out his revolver, began to shoot at it. The first two shots missed the bottle, but hit the pipe. The third shattered the bottle. I hoped that the young ruffian would be content; but he emptied the other barrels at the pipe, and one, skimming over the pipe, whistled through my hair as I crouched on the other side.

' 'Ware bridge!' a voice cried, to my relief.

Rupert and De Gautet cried, 'A moment!' and ran across. The bridge was drawn back, and all became still. The clock struck a quarter-past one. I rose and stretched myself and yawned.

I think some ten minutes had passed when I heard a slight noise to my right. I peered over the pipe, and saw a dark figure standing in the gateway that led to the bridge. It was a man. By the careless, graceful poise, I guessed it to be Rupert again. He held a sword in his hand, and he stood motionless for a minute or two. Wild thoughts ran through me. On what mischief was the young fiend bent now? Then he laughed low to himself; then he turned his face to the wall, took a step in my direction, and, to my surprise, began to climb down the wall. In an instant I saw that there must be steps in the wall; it was plain. They were cut into or affixed to the wall, at intervals of about eighteen inches. Rupert set his foot on the lower one. Then he placed his sword between his teeth, turned round, and noiselessly let himself down into the water. Had it been a matter of my life only, I would have swum to meet him. Dearly would I have loved to fight it out with him then and there—with steel, on a fine night and none to come between us. But there was the king! I restrained myself, but I could not bridle my swift breathing, and I watched him with the intensest eagerness.

He swam leisurely and quietly across. There were more foot-steps up on the other side, and he climbed them. When he set foot in the gateway, standing on the drawn-back bridge, he felt in his pocket and took something out. I heard him unlock the door. I could hear no noise of its closing behind him. He vanished from my sight.

Abandoning my ladder—I saw I did not need it now,—I swam to the side of the bridge, and climbed half-way up the steps. There I hung, with my sword in my hand, listening eagerly. The duke's room was shuttered and dark. There was a light in the window on the opposite side of the bridge. Not a sound broke the silence, till half-past one chimed from the great clock in the tower of the *château*.

There were other plots than mine afoot in the Castle that night.

CHAPTER XVIII

THE FORCING OF THE TRAP

THE position wherein I stood does not appear very favourable to thought; yet for the next moment or two I thought profoundly. I had, I told myself, scored one point. Be Rupert Hentzau's errand what it might, and the villainy he was engaged on what it would, I had scored one point. He was on the other side of the moat from the king, and it would be by no fault of mine if ever he set foot on the same side again. I had three left to deal with: two on guard and De Gautet in his bed. Ah, if I had the keys! I would have risked everything and attacked Detchard and Bersonin before their friends could join them. But I was powerless. I must wait till the coming of my friends enticed someone to cross the bridge—someone with the keys. And I waited, as it seemed, for half-an-hour, really for about five minutes, before the next act in the rapid drama began.

All was still on the other side. The duke's room remained inscrutable behind its shutters. The light burnt steadily in Madame de Mauban's window. Then I heard the faintest, faintest sound: it came from behind the door which led to the drawbridge on the other side of the moat. It but just reached my ear, yet I could not be mistaken as to what it was. It was made by a key being turned very carefully and slowly. Who was turning it? And of what room was it the key? There leapt before my eyes the picture of young Rupert, with the key in one hand, his sword in the other, and an evil smile on his face. But I did not know what door it was, nor on which of his favourite pursuits young Rupert was spending the hours of that night.

I was soon to be enlightened, for the next moment—before my friends could be near the *château* door—before Johann the keeper would have thought to nerve himself for his task—there was a sudden crash from the room with the lighted window. It sounded as though someone had flung down a lamp; and the window went dark and black. At the same instant a cry rang out, shrill in the night: 'Help, help! Michael, help!' and was followed by a shriek of utter terror.

I was tingling in every nerve. I stood on the topmost step, clinging to the threshold of the gate with my right hand and holding my sword in my left. Suddenly I perceived that the gateway was broader than the bridge; there was a dark corner on the opposite side where a man could stand. I darted across and stood there. Thus placed, I commanded the path, and no man could pass between the *château* and the old Castle till he had tried conclusions with me.

There was another shriek. Then a door was flung open and clanged against the wall, and I heard the handle of a door savagely twisted.

'Open the door! In God's name, what's the matter?' cried a voice—the voice of Black Michael himself.

He was answered by the very words I had written in my letter: 'Help, Michael—Hentzau!'

A fierce oath rang out from the duke, and with a loud thud he threw himself against the door. At the same moment I heard a window above my head open, and a voice cried: 'What's the matter?' and I heard a man's hasty footsteps. I grasped my sword. If De Gautet came my way, the Six would be less by one more.

Then I heard the clash of crossed swords and a tramp of feet, and—I cannot tell the thing so quickly as it happened, for all seemed to come at once. There was an angry cry from madame's room, the cry of a wounded man; the window was flung open; young Rupert stood there sword in hand. He turned his back, and I saw his body go forward to the lunge.

'Ah, Johann, there's one for you! Come on, Michael!'

Johann was there, then—come to the rescue of the duke! How would he open the door for me? For I feared that Rupert had slain him.

'Help!' cried the duke's voice, faint and husky.

I heard a step on the stairs above me; and I heard a stir down to my right, in the direction of the king's cell. But, before anything happened on my side of the moat, I saw five or six men round young Rupert in the embrasure of madame's window. Three or four times he lunged with incomparable dash and dexterity. For an instant they fell back, leaving a ring round him. He leapt on the parapet of the window, laughing as he leapt, and waving his sword in his hand. He was drunk with blood, and he laughed again wildly as he flung himself headlong into the moat.

What became of him then? I did not see: for as he leapt, De Gautet's lean face looked out through the door by me, and, without a second's hesitation, I struck at him with all the strength God had given me, and he fell dead in the doorway without a word or a groan. I dropped on my knees by him. Where were the keys? I found myself muttering: 'The keys, man, the keys?' as though he had been yet alive and could listen; and when I could not find them, I—God forgive me!—I believe I struck a dead man's face.

At last I had them. There were but three. Seizing the largest, I felt the lock of the door that led to the cell. I fitted in the key. It was right! The lock turned. I drew the door close behind me and locked it as noiselessly as I could, putting the key in my pocket.

I found myself at the top of a flight of steep stone stairs. An oil-lamp burnt dimly in the bracket. I took it down and held it in my hand; and I stood and listened.

'What in the devil can it be?' I heard a voice say.

It came from behind a door that faced me at the bottom of the stairs.

And another answered:

'Shall we kill him?'

I strained to hear the answer, and could have sobbed with relief when Detchard's voice came grating and cold:

'Wait a bit. There'll be trouble if we strike too soon.'

There was a moment's silence. Then I heard the bolt of the door cautiously drawn back. Instantly I put out the light I held, replacing the lamp in the bracket.

'It's dark—the lamp's out. Have you a light?' said the other voice—Bersonin's.

No doubt they had a light, but they should not use it. It was come to the crisis now, and I rushed down the steps and flung myself against the door. Bersonin had unbolted it and it gave way before me. The Belgian stood there sword in hand, and Detchard was sitting on a couch at the side of the room. In astonishment at seeing me, Bersonin recoiled; Detchard jumped to his sword. I rushed madly at the Belgian: he gave way before me, and I drove him up against the wall. He was no swordsman, though he fought bravely, and in a moment he lay on the floor before me. I turned—Detchard was not there. Faithful to his

orders, he had not risked a fight with me, but had rushed straight to
the door of the king's room, opened it and slammed it behind him.
Even now he was at his work inside.

And surely he would have killed the king, and perhaps me also, had
it not been for one devoted man who gave his life for the king. For
when I forced the door, the sight I saw was this. The king stood in the
corner of the room: broken by his sickness, he could do nothing; his
fettered hands moved uselessly up and down, and he was laughing
horribly in half-mad delirium. Detchard and the doctor were together
in the middle of the room; and the doctor had flung himself on the
murderer, pinning his hands to his sides for an instant. Then Detchard
wrenched himself free from the feeble grip and, as I entered, drove
his sword through the hapless man.

Then he turned on me, crying:

'At last!'

We were sword to sword. By blessed chance, neither he nor
Bersonin had been wearing their revolvers. I found them afterwards,
ready loaded, on the mantelpiece of the outer room: it was hard by the
door, ready to their hands, but my sudden rush in had cut off access
to them. Yes, we were man to man: and we began to fight, silently,
sternly, and hard. Yet I remember little of it, save that the man was my
match with the sword—nay, and more, for he knew more tricks than
I; and that he forced me back against the bars that guarded the entrance
to 'Jacob's Ladder'. And I saw a smile on his face, and he wounded me
in the left arm.

No glory do I take for that contest. I believe that the man would
have mastered me and slain me, and then done his butcher's work, for
he was the most skilful swordsman I have ever met; but even as he
pressed me hard, the half-mad, wasted, wan creature in the corner
leapt high in lunatic mirth, shrieking:

'It's cousin Rudolf! Cousin Rudolf! I'll help you, cousin Rudolf!'
and catching up a chair in his hands (he could but just lift it from the
ground and hold it uselessly before him) he came towards us. Hope
came to me.

'Come on!' I cried. 'Come on! Drive it against his legs.'

Detchard replied with a savage thrust. He all but had me.

'Come on! Come on, man!' I cried. 'Come and share the fun!'

And the king laughed gleefully, and came on, pushing his chair before him.

With an oath Detchard skipped back, and, before I knew what he was doing, had turned his sword against the king. He made one fierce cut at the king, and the king, with a piteous cry, dropped where he stood. The stout ruffian turned to face me again. But his own hand had prepared his destruction: for in turning, he trod in the pool of blood that flowed from the dead physician. He slipped; he fell. Like a dart I was upon him. I caught him by the throat, and before he could recover himself I drove my point through his neck, and with a stifled curse he fell across the body of his victim.

Was the king dead? It was my first thought. I rushed to where he lay. Ay, it seemed as if he were dead, for he had a great gash across the forehead, and he lay still in a huddled heap on the floor. I dropped on my knees beside him, and leant my ear down to hear if he breathed. But before I could, there was a loud rattle from the outside. I knew the sound: the drawbridge was being pushed out. A moment later it rang home against the wall on my side of the moat. I should be caught in a trap and the king with me, if he yet lived. He must take his chance, to live or to die. I took my sword, and passed into the outer room. Who were pushing the drawbridge out—my men? If so, all was well. My eye fell on the revolvers, and I seized one; and paused to listen in the doorway of the outer room. To listen, say I? Yes, and to get my breath: and I tore my shirt and twisted a strip of it round my bleeding arm; and stood listening again. I would have given the world to hear Sapt's voice. For I was faint, spent, and weary. And that wild-cat Rupert Hentzau was yet at large in the Castle. Yet, because I could better defend the narrow door at the top of the stairs than the wider entrance to the room, I dragged myself up the steps, and stood behind it listening.

What was the sound? Again a strange one for the place and the time. An easy, scornful, merry laugh—the laugh of young Rupert Hentzau! I could scarcely believe that a sane man would laugh. Yet the laugh told me that my men had not come; for they must have shot Rupert ere now, if they had come. And the clock struck half-past two! My God! The door had not been opened! They had gone to the bank! They had not found me! They had gone by now back to Tarlenheim, with the news of the king's death—and mine. Well, it would be true before they got there. Was not Rupert laughing in triumph?

For a moment I sank, unnerved, against the door. Then I started up alert again, for Rupert cried scornfully:

'Well, the bridge is there! Come over it! And in God's name, let's see Black Michael. Keep back, you curs! Michael, come and fight for her!'

If it were a three-cornered fight, I might yet bear my part. I turned the key in the door and looked out.

CHAPTER XIX

FACE TO FACE IN THE FOREST

FOR a moment I could see nothing, for the glare of lanterns and torches caught me full in the eyes from the other side of the bridge. But soon the scene grew clear: and it was a strange scene. The bridge was in its place. At the far end of it stood a group of the duke's servants; two or three carried the lights which had dazzled me, three or four held pikes in rest. They were huddled together; their weapons were protruded before them; their faces were pale and agitated. To put it plainly, they looked in as arrant a fright as I have seen men look, and they gazed apprehensively at a man who stood in the middle of the bridge, sword in hand. Rupert Hentzau was in his trousers and shirt; the white linen was stained with blood, but his easy, buoyant pose told me that he was himself either not touched at all or merely scratched. There he stood, holding the bridge against them, and daring them to come on; or, rather, bidding them send Black Michael to him; and they, having no firearms, cowered before the desperate man and dared not attack him. They whispered to one another; and, in the backmost rank, I saw my friend Johann, leaning against the portal of the door and stanching with a handkerchief the blood which flowed from a wound in his cheek.

By marvellous chance, I was master. The cravens would oppose me no more than they dared attack Rupert. I had but to raise my revolver, and I sent him to his account with his sins on his head. He did not so much as know that I was there. I did nothing—why I hardly know to this day. I had killed one man stealthily that night, and another by luck rather than skill—perhaps it was that. Again, villain as the man was, I did not relish being one of a crowd against him—perhaps it was that. But stronger than either of these restraining feelings came a curiosity and a fascination which held me spellbound, watching for the outcome of the scene.

'Michael, you dog! Michael! If you can stand, come on!' cried Rupert; and he advanced a step, the group shrinking back a little before him. 'Michael, you bastard! come on!'

The answer to his taunts came in the wild cry of a woman:
'He's dead! My God, he's dead!'

'Dead!' shouted Rupert. 'I struck better than I knew!' and he laughed triumphantly. Then he went on: 'Down with your weapons there! I'm your master now! Down with them, I say!'

I believe they would have obeyed, but as he spoke came new things. First, there arose a distant sound, as of shouts and knockings from the other side of the *château*. My heart leapt. It must be my men, come by a happy disobedience to seek me. The noise continued, but none of the rest seemed to heed it. Their attention was chained by what now happened before their eyes. The group of servants parted and a woman staggered on to the bridge. Antoinette de Mauban was in a loose white robe, her dark hair streamed over her shoulders, her face was ghastly pale, and her eyes gleamed wildly in the light of the torches. In her shaking hand she held a revolver, and, as she tottered forward, she fired it at Rupert Hentzau. The ball missed him, and struck the woodwork over my head.

'Faith, madame,' laughed Rupert, 'had your eyes been no more deadly than your shooting, I had not been in this scrape—nor Black Michael in hell—tonight!'

She took no notice of his words. With a wonderful effort, she calmed herself till she stood still and rigid. Then very slowly and deliberately she began to raise her arm again, taking most careful aim.

He would be mad to risk it. He must rush on her, chancing the bullet, or retreat towards me. I covered him with my weapon.

He did neither. Before she had got her aim, he bowed in his most graceful fashion, cried 'I can't kill where I've kissed,' and before she or I could stop him, laid his hand on the parapet of the bridge, and lightly leapt into the moat.

At the very moment I heard a rush of feet, and a voice I knew—Sapt's—cry: 'God! it's the duke—dead!' Then I knew that the king needed me no more, and, throwing down my revolver, I sprang out on the bridge. There was a cry of wild wonder, 'The king!' and then I, like Rupert Hentzau, sword in hand, vaulted over the parapet, intent on finishing my quarrel with him where I saw his curly head fifteen yards off in the water of the moat.

He swam swiftly and easily. I was weary and half-crippled with my wounded arm. I could not gain on him. For a time I made no sound, but as we rounded the corner of the old keep I cried:

'Stop, Rupert, stop!'

I saw him look over his shoulder, but he swam on. He was under the bank now, searching, as I guessed, for a spot that he could climb. I knew there to be none—but there was my rope, which would still be hanging where I had left it. He would come to where it was before I could. Perhaps he would miss it—perhaps he would find it; and if he drew it up after him, he would get a good start of me. I put forth all my remaining strength and pressed on. At last I began to gain on him; for he, occupied with his search, unconsciously slackened his pace.

Ah, he had found it! A low shout of triumph came from him. He laid hold of it and began to haul himself up. I was near enough to hear him mutter: 'How the devil comes this here?' I was at the rope, and he, hanging in mid-air, saw me; but I could not reach him.

'Hullo! who's here?' he cried in startled tones.

For a moment, I believe, he took me for the king—I daresay I was pale enough to lend colour to the thought; but an instant later he cried:

'Why, it's the play-actor! How came you here, man?'

And so saying, he gained the bank.

I laid hold of the rope, but I paused. He stood on the bank, sword in hand, and he could cut my head open or spit me through the heart as I came up. I let go the rope.

'Never mind,' said I; 'but as I am here, I think I'll stay.'

He smiled down on me.

'These women are the deuce——' he began; when suddenly the great bell of the Castle started to ring furiously, and a loud shout reached us from the moat.

Rupert smiled again, and waved his hand to me.

'I should like a turn with you, but it's a little too hot!' said he, and he disappeared from above me.

In an instant, without thinking of danger, I laid my hand to the rope. I was up. I saw him thirty yards off, running like a deer towards the shelter of the forest. For once Rupert Hentzau had chosen discretion for his part. I laid my feet to the ground and rushed after him, calling to him to stand. He would not. Unwounded and vigorous, he gained on me at every step; but, forgetting everything in the world except him and my thirst for his blood, I pressed on, and soon the deep shades of the forest of Zenda engulfed us both, pursued and pursuer.

It was three o'clock now, and day was dawning. I was on a long straight grass avenue, and a hundred yards ahead ran young Rupert, his curls waving in the fresh breeze. I was weary and panting; he looked over his shoulder and waved his hand again to me. He was mocking me, for he saw he had the pace of me. I was forced to pause for breath. A moment later, Rupert turned sharply to the right and was lost from my sight.

I thought all was over, and in deep vexation sank on the ground. But I was up again directly, for a scream rang through the forest—a woman's scream. Putting forth the last of my strength, I ran on to the place where he had turned out of my sight, and, turning also, I saw him again. But alas! I could not touch him. He was in the act of lifting a girl down from her horse; doubtless it was her scream that I heard. She looked like a small farmer's or a peasant's daughter, and she carried a basket on her arm. Probably she was on her way to the early market at Zenda. Her horse was a stout, well-shaped animal. Master Rupert lifted her down amid her shrieks—the sight of him frightened her; but he treated her gently, laughed, kissed her, and gave her money. Then he jumped on the horse, sitting sideways like a woman; and then he waited for me. I, on my part, waited for him.

Presently he rode towards me, keeping his distance however. He lifted up his hand, saying:

'What did you in the Castle?'

'I killed three of your friends,' said I.

'What! You got to the cells?'

'Yes.'

'And the king?'

'He was hurt by Detchard before I killed Detchard, but I pray that he lives.'

'You fool!' said Rupert, pleasantly.

'One thing more I did.'

'And what's that?'

'I spared your life. I was behind you on the bridge, with a revolver in my hand.'

'No? Faith, I was between two fires!'

'Get off your horse,' I cried, 'and fight like a man.'

'Before a lady!' said he, pointing to the girl. 'Fie, your Majesty!'

Then in my rage, hardly knowing what I did, I rushed at him. For a moment he seemed to waver. Then he reined his horse in and stood waiting for me. On I went in my folly. I seized the bridle and I struck at him. He parried and thrust at me. I fell back a pace and rushed in at him again; and this time I reached his face and laid his cheek open, and darted back before he could strike me. He seemed almost mazed at the fierceness of my attack; otherwise I think he must have killed me. I sank on my knee panting, expecting him to ride at me. And so he would have done, and then and there, I doubt not, one or both of us would have died; but at the moment there came a shout from behind us, and, looking round, I saw, just at the turn of the avenue, a man on a horse. He was riding hard, and he carried a revolver in his hand. It was Fritz von Tarlenheim, my faithful friend. Rupert saw him, and knew that the game was up. He checked his rush at me and flung his leg over the saddle, but yet for just a moment he waited. Leaning forward, he tossed his hair off his forehead and smiled, and said:

'*Au revoir*, Rudolf Rassendyll!'

Then, with his cheek streaming blood, but his lips laughing and his body swaying with ease and grace, he bowed to me; and he bowed to the farm-girl, who had drawn near in trembling fascination, and he waved his hand to Fritz, who was just within range and let fly a shot at him. The ball came nigh doing its work, for it struck the sword he held, and he dropped the sword with an oath, wringing his fingers, and clapped his heels hard on his horse's belly, and rode away at a gallop.

And I watched him go down the long avenue, riding as though he rode for his pleasure and singing as he went, for all there was that gash in his cheek.

Once again he turned to wave his hand, and then the gloom of the thickets swallowed him and he was lost from our sight. Thus he vanished—reckless and wary, graceful and graceless, handsome, debonair, vile, and unconquered. And I flung my sword passionately on the ground and cried to Fritz to ride after him. But Fritz stopped his horse, and leapt down and ran to me, and knelt, putting his arm about me. And indeed it was time, for the wound that Detchard had given me was broken forth afresh, and my blood was staining the ground.

'Then give me the horse!' I cried, staggering to my feet and throwing his arms off me. And the strength of my rage carried me so far as where the horse stood, and then I fell prone beside it. And Fritz knelt by me again.

'Fritz!' I said.

'Ay, friend—dear friend!' said he, tender as a woman.

'Is the king alive?'

He took his handkerchief and wiped my lips, and bent and kissed me on the forehead.

'Thanks to the most gallant gentleman that lives,' said he softly, 'the king is alive!'

The little farm-girl stood by us, weeping for fright and wide-eyed for wonder; for she had seen me at Zenda: and was not I, pallid, dripping, foul, and bloody as I was—yet was not I the king?

And when I heard that the king was alive, I strove to cry 'Hurrah!' But I could not speak, and I laid my head back in Fritz's arms and closed my eyes, and I groaned; and then, lest Fritz should do me wrong in his thoughts, I opened my eyes and tried to say 'Hurrah!' again. But I could not. And being very tired, and now very cold, I huddled myself close up to Fritz, to get the warmth of him, and shut my eyes again and went to sleep.

CHAPTER XX

THE PRISONER AND THE KING

In order to a full understanding of what had occurred in the Castle of Zenda, it is necessary to supplement my account of what I myself saw and did on that night by relating briefly what I afterwards learnt from Fritz and from Madame de Mauban. The story told by the latter explained clearly how it happened that the cry which I had arranged as a stratagem and a sham had come, in dreadful reality, before its time, and had thus, as it seemed at the moment, ruined our hopes, while in the end it had favoured them. The unhappy woman, fired, I believe, by a genuine attachment to the Duke of Strelsau, no less than by the dazzling prospects which a dominion over him opened before her eyes, had followed him at his request from Paris to Ruritania. He was a man of strong passions, but of stronger will, and his cool head ruled both. He was content to take all and give nothing. When she arrived, she was not long in finding that she had a rival in the Princess Flavia; rendered desperate, she stood at nothing which might give, or keep for her, her power over the duke. As I say, he took and gave not. Simultaneously, Antoinette found herself entangled in his audacious schemes. Unwilling to abandon him, bound to him by the chains of shame and hope, yet she would not be a decoy, nor, at his bidding, lure me to death. Hence the letters of warning she had written. Whether the lines she sent to Flavia were inspired by good or bad feeling, by jealousy or by pity, I do not know; but here also she served us well. When the duke went to Zenda, she accompanied him; and here for the first time she learnt the full measure of his cruelty, and was touched with compassion for the unfortunate king. From this time she was with us; yet, from what she told me, I know that she still (as women will) loved Michael, and trusted to gain his life, if not his pardon, from the king, as the reward for her assistance. His triumph she did not desire, for she loathed his crime, and loathed yet more fiercely what would be the prize of it—his marriage with his cousin, Princess Flavia.

At Zenda new forces came into play—the lust and daring of young Rupert. He was caught by her beauty, perhaps; perhaps it was enough for him that she belonged to another man, and that she hated him. For many days there had been quarrels and ill-will between him and the duke, and the scene which I had witnessed in the duke's room was but one of many. Rupert's proposals to me, of which she had, of course, been ignorant, in no way surprised her when I related them; she had herself warned Michael against Rupert, even when she was calling on me to deliver her from both of them. On this night, then, Rupert had determined to have his will. When she had gone to her room, he, having furnished himself with a key to it, had made his entrance. Her cries had brought the duke, and there in the dark room, while she screamed, the men had fought; and Rupert, having wounded his master with a mortal blow, had, on the servants rushing in, escaped through the window as I have described. The duke's blood, spurting out, had stained his opponent's shirt; but Rupert, not knowing that he had dealt Michael his death, was eager to finish the encounter. How he meant to deal with the other three of the band, I know not. I daresay he did not think, for the killing of Michael was not premeditated. Antoinette, left alone with the duke, had tried to stanch his wound, and thus was she busied till he died; and then, hearing Rupert's taunts, she had come forth to avenge him. Me she had not seen, nor did she till I darted out of my ambush, and leapt after Rupert into the moat.

The same moment found my friends on the scene. They had reached the *château* in due time, and waited ready by the door. But Johann, swept with the rest to the rescue of the duke, did not open it; nay, he took a part against Rupert, putting himself forward more bravely than any in his anxiety to avert suspicion; and he had received a wound, in the embrasure of the window. Till nearly half-past two Sapt waited; then, following my orders, he had sent Fritz to search the banks of the moat. I was not there. Hastening back, Fritz told Sapt; and Sapt was for following orders still, and riding at full speed back to Tarlenheim; while Fritz would not hear of abandoning me, let me have ordered what I would. On this they disputed some few minutes; then Sapt, persuaded by Fritz, detached a party under Bernenstein to gallop back to Tarlenheim and bring up the marshal, while the rest fell to on the great door of the *château*. For several minutes it resisted them; then, just as Antoinette de Mauban fired at Rupert Hentzau on the bridge, they broke in, eight of them in all: and the first door they came to was the door of Michael's room; and Michael lay dead across the threshold, with a sword-thrust through his breast. Sapt cried out at his death, as I had heard, and they rushed on the servants; but these, in fear, dropped their weapons, and Antoinette flung herself weeping at Sapt's feet. And all she cried was, that I had been at the end of the bridge and had leapt off. 'What of the prisoner?' asked Sapt; but she shook her head. Then Sapt and Fritz, with the gentlemen behind them, crossed the bridge, slowly, warily, and without noise; and Fritz stumbled over the body of De Gautet in the way of the door. They felt him and found him dead.

Then they consulted, listening eagerly for any sound from the cells below; but there came none, and they were greatly afraid that the king's guards had killed him, and having pushed his body through the great pipe, had escaped the same way themselves. Yet, because I had been seen here, they had still some hope (thus indeed Fritz, in his friendship, told me); and going back to Michael's body, pushing aside Antoinette, who prayed by it, they found a key to the door which I had locked, and opened the door. The staircase was dark, and they would not use a torch at first, lest they should be the more exposed to fire. But soon Fritz cried 'The door down there is open! See, there is light!' So they went on boldly, and found none to oppose them. And when they came to the outer room and saw the Belgian, Bersonin, lying dead, they thanked God, Sapt saying: 'Ay, he has been here.' Then rushing into the king's cell, they found Detchard lying dead across the dead physician, and the king on his back with his chair by him. And Fritz cried: 'He's dead!' and Sapt drove all out of the room except Fritz, and knelt down by the king; and, having learnt more of wounds and the signs of death than I, he soon knew that the king was not dead, nor, if properly attended, would die. And they covered his face and carried him to Duke Michael's room, and laid him there; and Antoinette rose from praying by the body of the duke and went to bathe the king's head and dress his wounds, till a doctor came. And Sapt, seeing I had been there, and having heard Antoinette's story, sent Fritz to search the moat and then the forest. He dared send no one else. And Fritz found my horse, and feared the worst. Then, as I have told, he found me, guided by the shout with which I had called

on Rupert to stop and face me. And I think a man has never been
more glad to find his own brother alive than was Fritz to come on me;
so that, in love and anxiety for me, he thought nothing of a thing so
great as would have been the death of Rupert Hentzau. Yet, had Fritz
killed him, I should have grudged it.

The enterprise of the king's rescue being thus prosperously con-
cluded, it lay on Colonel Sapt to secure secrecy as to the king ever
having been in need of rescue. Antoinette de Mauban and Johann
the keeper (who, indeed, was too much hurt to be wagging his
tongue just now) were sworn to reveal nothing; and Fritz went
forth to find—not the king, but the unnamed friend of the king,
who had lain in Zenda and flashed for a moment before the dazed
eyes of Duke Michael's servants on the drawbridge. The metamor-
phosis had happened; and the king, wounded almost to death by
the attacks of the gaolers who guarded his friend, had at last over-
come them, and rested now, wounded but alive, in Black Michael's
own room in the Castle. There he had been carried, his face covered
with a cloak, from the cell; and thence orders issued, that if his
friend were found, he should be brought directly and privately to
the king, and that meanwhile messengers should ride at full speed
to Tarlenheim, to tell Marshal Strakencz to assure the princess of
the king's safety, and to come himself with all speed to greet the king.
The princess was enjoined to remain at Tarlenheim, and there
await her cousin's coming or his further injunctions. Thus the king
would come to his own again, having wrought brave deeds, and
escaped, almost by a miracle, the treacherous assault of his unnatural
brother.

This ingenious arrangement of my long-headed old friend prospered
in every way, save where it encountered a force that often defeats the
most cunning schemes. I mean nothing else than the pleasure of
a woman. For, let her cousin and sovereign send what command he
chose (or Colonel Sapt chose for him), and let Marshal Strakencz
insist as he would, the Princess Flavia was in no way minded to rest at
Tarlenheim while her lover lay wounded at Zenda; and when the marshal, with a small *suite*,* rode forth from Tarlenheim on the way to
Zenda, the princess's carriage followed immediately behind, and in
this order they passed through the town, where the report was already

rife that the king, going the night before to remonstrate with his brother, in all friendliness, for that he held one of the king's friends in confinement in the Castle, had been most traitorously set upon; that there had been a desperate conflict; that the duke was slain with several of his gentlemen; and that the king, wounded as he was, had seized and held the Castle of Zenda. All of which talk made, as may be supposed, a mighty excitement; and the wires were set in motion, and the tidings came to Strelsau only just after orders had been sent thither to parade the troops and overawe the dissatisfied quarters of the town with a display of force.

Thus the Princess Flavia came to Zenda. And as she drove up the hill, with the marshal riding by the wheel and still imploring her to return in obedience to the king's orders, Fritz von Tarlenheim, with the prisoner of Zenda, came to the edge of the forest. I had revived from my swoon, and walked, resting on Fritz's arm; and looking out from the cover of the trees, I saw the princess. Suddenly understanding from a glance at my companion's face that we must not meet her, I sank on my knees behind a clump of bushes. But there was one whom we had forgotten, but who followed us, and was not disposed to let slip the chance of earning a smile and maybe a crown or two; and, while we lay hidden, the little farm-girl came by us and ran to the princess, curtseying and crying:

'Madame, the king is here—in the bushes! May I guide you to him, madame?'

'Nonsense, child!' said old Strakencz; 'the king lies wounded in the Castle.'

'Yes, sir, he's wounded, I know; but he's there—with Count Fritz—and not at the Castle,' she persisted.

'Is he in two places, or are there two kings?' asked Flavia, bewildered. 'And how should he be here?'

'He pursued a gentleman, madame, and they fought till Count Fritz came; and the other gentleman took my father's horse from me and rode away; but the king is here with Count Fritz. Why, madame, is there another man in Ruritania like the king?'

'No, my child,' said Flavia softly (I was told it afterwards), and she smiled and gave the girl money. 'I will go and see this gentleman,' and she rose to alight from the carriage.

But at this moment Sapt came riding from the Castle, and, seeing the princess, made the best of a bad job, and cried to her that the king was well tended and in no danger.

'In the Castle?' she asked.

'Where else, madame?' said he, bowing.

'But this girl says he is yonder—with Count Fritz.'

Sapt turned his eyes on the child with an incredulous smile.

'Every fine gentleman is a king to such,' said he.

'Why, he's as like the king as one pea to another, madame!' cried the girl, a little shaken but still obstinate.

Sapt started round. The old marshal's face asked unspoken questions. Flavia's glance was no less eloquent. Suspicion spreads quick.

'I'll ride myself and see this man,' said Sapt, hastily.

'Nay, I'll come myself,' said the princess.

'Then come alone,' he whispered.

And she, obedient to the strange hinting in his face, prayed the marshal and the rest to wait; and she and Sapt came on foot towards where we lay, Sapt waving to the farm-girl to keep at a distance. And when I saw them coming, I sat in a sad heap on the ground, and buried my face in my hands. I could not look at her. Fritz knelt by me, laying his hand on my shoulder.

'Speak low, whatever you say,' I heard Sapt whisper as they came up; and the next thing I heard was a low cry—half of joy, half of fear—from the princess:

'It is he! Are you hurt?'

And she fell on the ground by me, and gently pulled my hands away; but I kept my eyes to the ground.

'It is the king!' she said. 'Pray, Colonel Sapt, tell me where lay the wit of the joke you played on me?'

We answered, none of us: we three were silent before her. Regardless of them, she threw her arms round my neck and kissed me. Then Sapt spoke in a low hoarse whisper:

'It is not the king. Don't kiss him; he's not the king.'

She drew back for a moment; then, with an arm still round my neck, she asked, in superb indignation:

'Do I not know my love? Rudolf, my love!'

'It is not the king,' said old Sapt again; and a sudden sob broke from tender-hearted Fritz.

It was the sob that told her no comedy was afoot.

'He is the king!' she cried. 'It is the king's face—the king's ring—my ring! It is my love!'

'Your love, madame,' said old Sapt, 'but not the king. The king is there in the Castle. This gentleman——'

'Look at me, Rudolf! look at me!' she cried, taking my face between her hands. 'Why do you let them torment me? Tell me what it means!'

Then I spoke, gazing into her eyes.

'God forgive me, madame!' I said. 'I am not the king!'

I felt her hands clutch my cheeks. She gazed at me as never man's face was scanned yet. And I, silent again, saw wonder born, and doubt grow, and terror spring to life as she looked. And very gradually the grasp of her hands slackened: she turned to Sapt, to Fritz, and back to me: then suddenly she reeled forward and fell in my arms: and with a great cry of pain I gathered her to me and kissed her lips. Sapt laid his hand on my arm. I looked up in his face. And I laid her softly on the ground, and stood up, looking on her, cursing heaven that young Rupert's sword had spared me for this sharper pang.

CHAPTER XXI

IF LOVE WERE ALL!

It was night, and I was in the cell wherein the king had lain in the Castle of Zenda. The great pipe that Rupert of Hentzau had nicknamed 'Jacob's Ladder' was gone, and the lights in the room across the moat twinkled in the darkness. All was still; the din and clash of strife were gone. I had spent the day hidden in the forest, from the time when Fritz had led me off, leaving Sapt with the princess. Under cover of dusk, muffled up, I had been brought to the Castle and lodged where I now lay. Though three men had died there—two of them by my hand,—I was not troubled by ghosts. I had thrown myself on a pallet by the window, and was looking out on the black water; Johann the keeper, still pale from his wound, but not much hurt besides, had brought me supper. He told me that the king was doing well, that he had seen the princess; that she and he, Sapt and Fritz, had been long together. Marshal Strakencz was gone to Strelsau: Black Michael lay in his coffin, and Antoinette de Mauban watched by him; had I not heard, from the chapel, priests singing mass for him?

Outside there were strange rumours afloat. Some said that the prisoner of Zenda was dead; some, that he had vanished yet alive; some, that he was a friend who had served the king well in some adventure in England; others, that he had discovered the duke's plots, and had therefore been kidnapped by him. One or two shrewd fellows shook their heads and said only that they would say nothing, but they had suspicions that more was to be known than was known, if Colonel Sapt would tell all he knew.

Thus Johann chattered till I sent him away and lay there alone, thinking, not of the future, but—as a man is wont to do when stirring things have happened to him—rehearsing the events of the past weeks, and wondering how strangely they had fallen out. And above me, in the stillness of the night, I heard the standards flapping against their poles, for Black Michael's banner hung there half-mast high, and above it the royal flag of Ruritania, floating for one night more over my head. Habit grows so quick, that only by an effort did I recollect that it floated no longer for me.

Presently Fritz von Tarlenheim came into the room. I was standing then by the window; the glass was opened, and I was idly fingering the cement which clung to the masonry where 'Jacob's Ladder' had been. He told me briefly that the king wanted me, and together we crossed the drawbridge and entered the room that had been Black Michael's.

The king was lying there in bed; our doctor from Tarlenheim was in attendance on him, and whispered to me that my visit must be brief. The king held out his hand and shook mine. Fritz and the doctor withdrew to the window.

I took the king's ring from my finger and placed it on his.

'I have tried not to dishonour it, sire,' said I.

'I can't talk much to you,' he said, in a weak voice. 'I have had a great fight with Sapt and the marshal—for we have told the marshal everything. I wanted to take you to Strelsau and keep you with me, and tell everyone of what you had done; and you would have been my best and nearest friend, Cousin Rudolf. But they tell me I must not, and that the secret must be kept—if kept it can be.'

'They are right, sire. Let me go. My work here is done.'

'Yes, it is done, as no man but you could have done it. When they see me again, I shall have my beard on; I shall—yes, faith, I shall be wasted with sickness. They will not wonder that the king looks changed in face. Cousin, I shall try to let them find him changed in nothing else. You have shown me how to play the king.'

'Sire,' said I, 'I can take no praise from you. It is by the narrowest grace of God that I was not a worse traitor than your brother.'

He turned inquiring eyes on me; but a sick man shrinks from puzzles, and he had no strength to question me. His glance fell on Flavia's ring, which I wore. I thought he would question me about it; but, after fingering it idly, he let his head fall on his pillow.

'I don't know when I shall see you again,' he said faintly, almost listlessly.

'If I can ever serve you again, sire,' I answered.

His eyelids closed. Fritz came with the doctor. I kissed the king's hand, and let Fritz lead me away. I have never seen the king since.

Outside, Fritz turned, not to the right, back towards the draw-bridge, but to the left, and, without speaking, led me upstairs, through a handsome corridor in the *château*.

'Where are we going?' I asked.

Looking away from me, Fritz answered:

'She has sent for you. When it is over, come back to the bridge. I'll wait for you there.'

'What does she want?' said I, breathing quickly.

He shook his head.

'Does she know everything?'

'Yes, everything.'

He opened a door, and gently pushing me in, closed it behind me. I found myself in a drawing-room, small and richly furnished. At first I thought that I was alone, for the light that came from a pair of shaded candles on the mantelpiece was very dim. But presently I discerned a woman's figure standing by the window. I knew it was the princess, and I walked up to her, fell on one knee, and carried the hand that hung by her side to my lips. She neither moved nor spoke. I rose to my feet, and, piercing the gloom with my eager eyes, saw her pale face and the gleam of her hair, and before I knew, I spoke softly:

'Flavia!'

She trembled a little, and looked round. Then she darted to me, taking hold of me.

'Don't stand, don't stand! No, you mustn't! You're hurt! Sit down—here, here!'

She made me sit on a sofa, and put her hand on my forehead.

'How hot your head is,' she said, sinking on her knees by me. Then she laid her head against me, and I heard her murmur: 'My darling, how hot your head is!'

Somehow love gives even to a dull man the knowledge of his lover's heart. I had come to humble myself and pray pardon for my presumption; but what I said now was:

'I love you with all my heart and soul!'

For what troubled and shamed her? Not her love for me, but the fear that I had counterfeited the lover as I had acted the king, and taken her kisses with a smothered smile.

'With all my life and heart!' said I, as she clung to me. 'Always, from the first moment I saw you in the Cathedral! There has been but one woman in the world to me—and there will be no other. But God forgive me the wrong I've done you!'

'They made you do it!' she said quickly; and she added, raising her head and looking in my eyes: 'It might have made no difference if I'd known it. It was always you, never the king!' and she raised herself and kissed me.

'I meant to tell you,' said I. 'I was going to on the night of the ball in Strelsau, when Sapt interrupted me. After that, I couldn't—I couldn't risk losing you before—before—I must! My darling, for you I nearly left the king to die!'

'I know, I know! What are we to do now, Rudolf?'

I put my arm round her and held her up while I said:

'I am going away tonight.'

'Ah, no, no!' she cried. 'Not tonight!'

'I must go tonight, before more people have seen me. And how would you have me stay, sweetheart, except——'

'If I could come with you!' she whispered very low.

'My God!' said I roughly, 'don't talk about that!' and I thrust her a little back from me.

'Why not? I love you. You are as good a gentleman as the king!'

Then I was false to all that I should have held by. For I caught her in my arms and prayed her, in words that I will not write, to come with me, daring all Ruritania to take her from me. And for a while she listened, with wondering, dazzled eyes. But as her eyes looked upon me, I grew ashamed, and my voice died away in broken murmurs and stammerings, and at last I was silent.

She drew herself away from me and stood against the wall, while I sat on the edge of the sofa, trembling in every limb, knowing what I had done—loathing it, obstinate not to undo it. So we rested a long time.

'I am mad!' I said sullenly.

'I love your madness, dear,' she answered.

Her face was away from me, but I caught the sparkle of a tear on her cheek. I clutched the sofa with my hand and held myself there.

'Is love the only thing?' she asked, in low, sweet tones that seemed to bring a calm even to my wrung heart. 'If love were the only thing,

I would follow you—in rags, if need be—to the world's end; for you hold my heart in the hollow of your hand! But is love the only thing?'

I made her no answer. It gives me shame now to think that I would not help her.

She came near me and laid her hand on my shoulder. I put my hand up and held hers.

'I know people write and talk as if it were. Perhaps, for some, Fate lets it be. Ah, if I were one of them! But if love had been the only thing, you would have let the king die in his cell.'

I kissed her hand.

'Honour binds a woman too, Rudolf. My honour lies in being true to my country and my House. I don't know why God has let me love you; but I know that I must stay.'

Still I said nothing; and she, pausing a while, then went on:

'Your ring will always be on my finger, your heart in my heart, the touch of your lips on mine. But you must go, and I must stay. Perhaps I must do what it kills me to think of doing.'

I knew what she meant, and a shiver ran through me. But I could not utterly fail beside her. I rose and took her hand.

'Do what you will, or what you must,' I said. 'I think God shows his purposes to such as you. My part is lighter; for your ring shall be on my finger and your heart in mine, and no touch save of your lips will ever be on mine. So, may God comfort you, my darling!'

There struck on our ears the sound of singing. The priests in the chapel were singing masses for the souls of those who lay dead. They seemed to chant a requiem over our buried joy, to pray forgiveness for our love that would not die. The soft, sweet, pitiful music rose and fell as we stood opposite one another, her hands in mine.

'My queen and my beauty!' said I.

'My lover and true knight!' she said. 'Perhaps we shall never see one another again. Kiss me, my dear, and go!'

I kissed her as she bade me; but at the last she clung to me, whispering nothing but my name, and that over and over again—and again—and again; and then I left her.

Rapidly I walked down to the bridge. Sapt and Fritz were waiting for me. Under their directions I changed my dress, and muffling my face, as I had done more than once before, I mounted with them at the door of the Castle, and we three rode through the night and on to the breaking of day, and found ourselves at a little roadside station just over the border of Ruritania. The train was not quite due, and I walked with them in a meadow by a little brook while we waited for it. They promised to send me all news; they overwhelmed me with kindness—even old Sapt was touched to gentleness, while Fritz was half-unmanned. I listened in a kind of dream to all they said. 'Rudolf! Rudolf! Rudolf!' still rang in my ears—a burden of sorrow and of love. At last they saw that I could not heed them, and we walked up and down in silence, till Fritz touched me on the arm, and I saw, a mile or more away, the blue smoke of the train. Then I held out a hand to each of them.

'We are all but half-men this morning,' said I, smiling. 'But we have been men, eh, Sapt and Fritz, old friends? We have run a good course between us.'

'We have defeated traitors and set the king firm on his throne,' said Sapt.

Then Fritz von Tarlenheim suddenly, before I could discern his purpose or stay him, uncovered his head and bent as he used to do, and kissed my hand; and, as I snatched it away, he said, trying to laugh:

'Heaven doesn't always make the right men kings!'

Old Sapt twisted his mouth as he wrung my hand.

'The devil has his share in most things,' said he.

The people at the station looked curiously at the tall man with the muffled face, but we took no notice of their glances. I stood with my two friends, and waited till the train came up to us. Then we shook hands again, saying nothing; and both this time—and, indeed, from old Sapt it seemed strange—bared their heads, and so stood still till the train bore me away from their sight. So that it was thought some great man travelled privately for his pleasure from the little station that morning; whereas, in truth, it was only I, Rudolf Rassendyll, an English gentleman, a cadet* of a good house, but a man of no wealth nor position, nor of much rank. They would have been disappointed to know that. Yet had they known all, they would have looked more curiously still. For, be I what I might now, I had been for three months a king; which, if not a thing to be proud of, is at least an experience to have undergone. Doubtless I should have thought more of it, had there not echoed through the air, from the towers of Zenda that we were leaving far away, into my ears and into my heart the cry of a woman's love—'Rudolf! Rudolf! Rudolf!'

Hark! I hear it now!

CHAPTER XXII

PRESENT, PAST—AND FUTURE?

THE details of my return home can have but little interest. I went straight to the Tyrol and spent a quiet fortnight—mostly on my back, for a severe chill developed itself; and I was also the victim of a nervous reaction, which made me weak as a baby. As soon as I had reached my quarters, I sent an apparently careless postcard to my brother, announcing my good health and prospective return. That would serve to satisfy the enquiries as to my whereabouts, which were probably still vexing the Prefect of the Police of Strelsau. I let my moustache and imperial grow again; and as hair comes quickly on my face, they were respectable, though not luxuriant, by the time that I landed myself in Paris and called on my friend George Featherly. My interview with him was chiefly remarkable for the number of unwilling but necessary falsehoods that I told; and I rallied him unmercifully when he told me that he had made up his mind that I had gone in the track of Madame de Mauban to Strelsau. The lady, it appeared, was back in Paris but was living in great seclusion—a fact for which gossip found no difficulty in accounting. Did not all the world know of the treachery and death of Duke Michael? Nevertheless, George bade Bertram Bertrand be of good cheer, 'for,' said he flippantly, 'a live poet is better than a dead duke.' Then he turned on me and asked:

'What have you been doing to your moustache?'

'To tell the truth,' I answered, assuming a sly air, 'a man now and then has reasons for wishing to alter his appearance. But it's coming on very well again.'

'What? Then I wasn't so far out! If not the fair Antoinette, there was a charmer?'

'There is always a charmer,' said I, sententiously.

But George would not be satisfied till he had wormed out of me (he took much pride in his ingenuity) an absolutely imaginary love-affair, attended with the proper *soupçon* of scandal, which had kept me all this time in the peaceful regions of the Tyrol. In return for this narrative, George regaled me with a great deal of what he called 'inside information' (known only to diplomatists), as to the true course of events in Ruritania, the plots and counter-plots. In his opinion, he told me, with a significant nod, there was more to be said for Black Michael than the public supposed; and he hinted at a well-founded suspicion that the mysterious prisoner of Zenda, concerning whom a good many paragraphs had appeared, was not a man at all, but (here I had some ado not to smile) a woman disguised as a man; and that strife between the king and his brother for this imaginary lady's favour was at the bottom of their quarrel.

'Perhaps it was Madame de Mauban herself,' I suggested.

'No!' said George decisively. 'Antoinette de Mauban was jealous of her, and betrayed the duke to the king for that reason. And, to confirm what I say, it's well known that the Princess Flavia is now extremely cold to the king, after having been most affectionate.'

At this point I changed the subject, and escaped from George's 'inspired' delusions. But if diplomatists never know anything more than they had succeeded in finding out in this instance, they appear to me to be somewhat expensive luxuries.

While in Paris I wrote to Antoinette, though I did not venture to call upon her. I received in return a very affecting letter, in which she assured me that the king's generosity and kindness, no less than her regard for me, bound her conscience to absolute secrecy. She expressed the intention of settling in the country, and withdrawing herself entirely from society. Whether she carried out her designs, I have never heard; but as I have not met her, or heard news of her up to this time, it is probable that she did. There is no doubt that she was deeply attached to the Duke of Strelsau; and her conduct at the time of his death proved that no knowledge of the man's real character was enough to root her regard for him out of her heart.

I had one more battle left to fight—a battle that would, I knew, be severe, and was bound to end in my complete defeat. Was I not back from the Tyrol, without having made any study of its inhabitants, institutions, scenery, fauna, flora, or other features? Had I not simply wasted my time in my usual frivolous, good-for-nothing way? That was the aspect of the matter which, I was obliged to admit, would present itself to my sister-in-law; and against a verdict based on such evidence, I had really no defence to offer. It may be supposed, then, that I presented myself in Park Lane in a shame-faced, sheepish fashion. On the whole, my reception was not so alarming as I had feared. It turned out that I had done, not what Rose wished, but—the next best thing—what she prophesied. She had declared that I should make no notes, record no observations, gather no materials. My brother, on the other hand, had been weak enough to maintain that a really serious resolve had at length animated me.

When I returned empty-handed, Rose was so occupied in triumphing over Burlesdon that she let me down quite easily, devoting the greater part of her reproaches to my failure to advertise my friends of my whereabouts.

'We've wasted a lot of time trying to find you,' she said.

'I know you have,' said I. 'Half our ambassadors have led weary lives on my account. George Featherly told me so. But why should you have been anxious? I can take care of myself.'

'Oh, it wasn't that,' she cried scornfully; 'but I wanted to tell you about Sir Jacob Borrodaile. You know, he's got an Embassy—at least, he will have in a month—and he wrote to say he hoped you would go with him.'

'Where's he going to?'

'He's going to succeed Lord Topham at Strelsau,' said she. 'You couldn't have a nicer place, short of Paris.'

'Strelsau! H'm!' said I, glancing at my brother.

'Oh, *that* doesn't matter!' exclaimed Rose, impatiently. 'Now, you will go, won't you?'

'I don't know that I care about it!'

'Oh, you're too exasperating!'

'And I don't think I can go to Strelsau. My dear Rose, would it be—suitable?'

'Oh, nobody remembers that horrid old story now.'

Upon this, I took out of my pocket a portrait of the King of Ruritania. It had been taken a month or two before he ascended the throne. She could not miss my point when I said, putting it into her hands:

'In case you've not seen, or not noticed, a picture of Rudolf V., there he is. Don't you think they might recall the story, if I appeared at the Court of Ruritania?'

My sister-in-law looked at the portrait, and then at me.

'Good gracious!' she said, and flung the photograph down on the table.

'What do you say, Bob?' I asked.

Burlesdon got up, went to a corner of the room, and searched in a heap of newspapers. Presently he came back with a copy of the *Illustrated London News*.* Opening the paper, he displayed a double-page engraving of the Coronation of Rudolf V. at Strelsau. The photograph and the picture he laid side by side. I sat at the table fronting them; and, as I looked, I grew absorbed. My eye travelled from my own portrait to Sapt, to Strakencz, to the rich robes of the Cardinal, to Black Michael's face, to the stately figure of the princess by his side. Long I looked and eagerly. I was roused by my brother's hand on my shoulder. He was gazing down at me with a puzzled expression.

'It's a remarkable likeness, you see,' said I. 'I really think I had better not go to Ruritania.'

Rose, though half convinced, would not abandon her position.

'It's just an excuse,' she said pettishly. 'You don't want to do anything. Why, you might become an ambassador!'

'I don't think I want to be an ambassador,' said I.

'It's more than you ever will be,' she retorted.

That is very likely true, but it is not more than I have been. The idea of being an ambassador could scarcely dazzle me. I had been a king!

So pretty Rose left us in dudgeon; and Burlesdon, lighting a cigarette, looked at me still with that curious gaze.

'That picture in the paper——' he said.

'Well, what of it? It shows that the King of Ruritania and your humble servant are as like as two peas.'

My brother shook his head.

'I suppose so,' he said. 'But I should know you from the man in the photograph.'

'And not from the picture in the paper?'

'I should know the photograph from the picture: the picture's very like the photograph, but——'

'Well?'

'It's more like you,' said my brother.

My brother is a good man and true—so that, for all that he is a married man and mighty fond of his wife, he should know any secret of mine. But this secret was not mine, and I could not tell it to him.

'I don't think it's so much like me as the photograph,' said I boldly. 'But, anyhow, Bob, I won't go to Strelsau.'

'No, don't go to Strelsau, Rudolf,' said he.

And whether he suspects anything, or has a glimmer of the truth, I do not know. If he has, he keeps it to himself, and he and I never refer to it. And we let Sir Jacob Borrodaile find another *attaché*.

Since all these events whose history I have set down happened, I have lived a very quiet life at a small house which I have taken in the country. The ordinary ambitions and aims of men in my position seem to me dull and unattractive. I have little fancy for the whirl of society, and none for the jostle of politics. Lady Burlesdon utterly despairs of me; my neighbours think me an indolent, dreamy, unsociable fellow. Yet I am a young man; and sometimes I have a fancy—the superstitious would call it a presentiment—that my part in life is not yet altogether played; that, somehow and some day, I shall mix again in great affairs, I shall again spin policies in a busy brain, match my wits against my enemies', brace my muscles to fight a good fight and strike stout blows. Such is the tissue of my thoughts as, with gun or rod in hand, I wander through the woods or by the side of the stream. Whether the fancy will be fulfilled, I cannot tell—still less whether the scene that, led by memory, I lay for my new exploits will be the true one—for I love to see myself once again in the crowded streets of Strelsau, or beneath the frowning keep of the Castle of Zenda.

Thus led, my broodings leave the future, and turn back on the past. Shapes rise before me in long array—the wild first revel with the king, the rush with my brave tea-table, the night in the moat, the pursuit in the forest: my friends and my foes, the people who learnt to love and honour me, the desperate men who tried to kill me. And, from amidst these last, comes one who alone of all of them yet moves on earth, though where I know not, yet plans (as I do not doubt) wickedness, yet turns women's hearts to softness and men's to fear and hate. Where is young Rupert of Hentzau—the boy who came so nigh to beating me? When his name comes into my head, I feel my hand grip and the blood move quicker through my veins: and the hint of Fate—the presentiment—seems to grow stronger and more definite, and to whisper insistently in my ear that I have yet a hand to play with young Rupert; therefore I exercise myself in arms, and seek to put off the day when the vigour of youth must leave me.

One break comes every year in my quiet life. Then I go to Dresden, and there I am met by my dear friend and companion, Fritz von Tarlenheim. Last time, his pretty wife Helga came, and a lusty crowing baby with her. And for a week Fritz and I are together, and I hear all of what falls out in Strelsau; and in the evenings, as we walk and smoke together, we talk of Sapt, and of the king, and often of young Rupert; and, as the hours grow small, at last we speak of Flavia. For every year Fritz carries with him to Dresden a little box; in it lies a red rose, and round the stalk of the rose is a slip of paper with the words written: 'Rudolf—Flavia—always.' And the like I send back by him. That message, and the wearing of the rings, are all that now bind me and the Queen of Ruritania. For—nobler, as I hold her, for the act—she has followed where her duty to her country and her House led her, and is the wife of the king, uniting his subjects to him by the love they bear to her, giving peace and quiet days to thousands by her self-sacrifice. There are moments when I dare not think of it, but there are others when I rise in spirit to where she ever dwells; then I can thank God that I love the noblest lady in the world, the most gracious and beautiful, and that there was nothing in my love that made her fall short in her high duty.

Shall I see her face again—the pale face and the glorious hair? Of that I know nothing; Fate has no hint, my heart no presentiment. I do not know. In this world, perhaps—nay, it is likely—never. And can it be that somewhere, in a manner whereof our flesh-bound minds have no apprehension, she and I will be together again, with nothing to come between us, nothing to forbid our love? That I know not, nor wiser heads than mine. But if it be never—if I can never hold sweet converse again with her, or look upon her face, or know from her her love; why, then, this side the grave, I will live as becomes the man whom she loves; and, for the other side, I must pray a dreamless sleep.

THE END

EXPLANATORY NOTES

6 *305 Park Lane, W.*: Park Lane lies between Mayfair and Hyde Park in London. Now dominated by luxury hotels, in the late nineteenth century it was the site of some of the city's grandest private houses.

7 *this heredity . . . about*: the inheritance of physical and mental traits is a significant topic in the novels of the period, for example, Thomas Hardy's *Tess of the d'Urbervilles* (1891), H. G. Wells's *The Time Machine* (1895), and Arthur Conan Doyle's *The Hound of the Baskervilles* (1901–2).

a German school and a German University: Germany was to the forefront of academic reform, and attracted many international students, but Rassendyll's education also equips him well for his adventure in German-speaking Ruritania.

8 *two thousand pounds a year*: a very large income at a time when an adult male manual labourer or a junior clerk might earn £50 a year, and an experienced clerk £200–300.

9 *the Tyrol*: at this time an Alpine region of the Austro-Hungarian Empire.

11 *'The Continental'*: now the Westin Paris-Vendôme, the luxurious Hotel Continental was completed in 1878, indicating that the story is set in the recent past.

Durand's: the Café Durand was a celebrated restaurant on the corner of the Place de la Madeleine in Paris.

The Critic: presumably a fictitious publication, though there was an American magazine of that name (1881–1906).

12 *morganatic marriage*: a marriage between a titled individual and someone of lower status in which neither the spouse nor their offspring acquires a title or rights of inheritance.

Dresden: in Saxony, in eastern Germany. This is the strongest hint we have of the approximate location of Ruritania. It had a famous picture gallery.

15 *Flavia*: originally a Roman name, from the Latin *flavus*, flaxen-haired.

19 *carefully pointed imperial*: 'A small pointed beard growing beneath the lower lip' (*OED*), chiefly associated with Emperor Napoleon III of France.

22 *sans phrase*: 'without more words . . . without exceptions or qualifications' (*OED*).

29 *'Lord, he's a heretic!'*: presumably Rassendyll is an Anglican.

30 *Drain your flask, Fritz*: Fritz carries a hip flask filled with brandy, or some other spirit.

31 *aide-de-camp*: an assistant, usually an officer who assists an officer of higher rank.

32 *Cuirassiers*: cavalry wearing light armour.

34 *archiepiscopal throne*: that of an archbishop.

39 *princes of the blood*: as the child of a morganatic marriage, Michael is not a prince.

41 *whom I knew well . . . Max Holf*: presumably this should read 'whom I knew well afterwards', since Rassendyll has not met Holf.

45 *personate*: impersonate.

48 *partie carrée*: a foursome.

50 *'Osric' in Hamlet*: a somewhat verbose courtier who appears in Act 5 Scene ii.

51 *'making my mark'*: signing a document with an x or similar mark.

corps diplomatique: the foreign diplomats at the Ruritanian court.

The Critic: Richard Brinsley Sheridan's 1779 burlesque. The comic stalemate occurs in Act 3 Scene i.

54 *You are . . . transformed by becoming king*: the prince in question is the rakish Prince Hal in *Henry IV Part 1* and *Henry IV Part 2*, who is transformed by becoming Henry V.

55 *of the Blood*: Flavia is in the direct line of succession. She will reign if the king dies.

57 *I spoke to him in English*: one of the few reminders that Rassendyll is otherwise speaking in German.

58 *cat's-cradle*: 'A children's game in which two players alternately take from each other's fingers an intertwined cord so as always to produce a symmetrical figure' (*OED*).

59 *Scylla . . . and Charybdis*: positioned between equally unattractive alternatives. In Greek legend the names of a sea monster and a whirlpool. (Misspelt 'Charbydis' in the first edition.)

62 *a bull's-eye lantern*: a lantern that could produce a focused beam of light.

65 *snap shot*: a shot fired without taking aim.

67 *écarté*: a trick-based card game for two players that uses a thirty-two-card deck.

68 *make love to her*: court her.

69 *quadrille*: a dance usually performed by four couples, not unlike an American square dance or Irish set dance.

71 *toils*: nets.

74 *nosegay*: a small bouquet.

inamorata: female lover.

81 *demesne*: the estate around the chateau.

boars . . . considerable numbers: in contrast with England, where boars had been extinct since the seventeenth century, Ruritania remains a wild place.

86 *Our little Delilah . . . Samson*: in Judges 16 Delilah is loved by the Israelite leader Samson, but is bribed by his enemies, the Philistines, to discover the secret of his great strength. When he reveals that it his hair that gives him his strength, she has it cut, and he is captured, blinded, and enslaved.

92 *corps*: body of troops.

93 *ladder of Jacob*: in Genesis 28 Jacob has a dream in which he sees a ladder between heaven and earth on which angels ascend and descend.

95 *clinched*: driven home.

99 *cooked*: done for, defeated.

102 *dans cette galère*: in this company or predicament; literally in this galley. The phrase comes from Molière's 1671 play, *Les Fourberies de Scapin*, Act 2 Scene vii.

106 *mal à propos*: at an inopportune moment.

114 *'Nil Quae Feci'*: Latin motto which can be translated as 'What I have done is nothing'.

136 *suite*: entourage.

145 *cadet*: the younger son in a family.

150 *Illustrated London News*: an illustrated weekly paper founded in 1842.

American Literature

British and Irish Literature

Children's Literature

Classics and Ancient Literature

Colonial Literature

Eastern Literature

European Literature

Gothic Literature

History

Medieval Literature

Oxford English Drama

Philosophy

Poetry

Politics

Religion

The Oxford Shakespeare

A complete list of Oxford World's Classics, including Authors in Context, Oxford English Drama, and the Oxford Shakespeare, is available in the UK from the Marketing Services Department, Oxford University Press, Great Clarendon Street, Oxford OX2 6DP, or visit the website at www.oup.com/uk/worldsclassics.

In the USA, visit www.oup.com/us/owc for a complete title list.

Oxford World's Classics are available from all good bookshops. In case of difficulty, customers in the UK should contact Oxford University Press Bookshop, 116 High Street, Oxford OX1 4BR.

ANTHONY TROLLOPE

The American Senator
An Autobiography
Barchester Towers
Can You Forgive Her?
Cousin Henry
Doctor Thorne
The Duke's Children
The Eustace Diamonds
Framley Parsonage
He Knew He Was Right
Lady Anna
The Last Chronicle of Barset
Orley Farm
Phineas Finn
Phineas Redux
The Prime Minister
Rachel Ray
The Small House at Allington
The Warden
The Way We Live Now